Austin Entertains

The Junior League of Austin

Austin
Entertains

★

The Junior League of Austin

Austin *Entertains*

Library of Congress Number: 00-134932
ISBN: 0-9605906-0-9

Designed, Edited, and Manufactured by
Favorite Recipes® Press
an imprint of

FRP

P.O. Box 305142
Nashville, Tennessee 37230
800-358-0560

Project Manager: Debbie Van Mol, RD
Art Director: Steve Newman

Manufactured in the United States of America
First Printing: 2001   30,000 copies

Mission Statement

The Junior League of Austin is an organization of women committed to promoting voluntarism, developing the potential of women, and improving the community through the effective action and leadership of trained volunteers. Its purpose is exclusively educational and charitable.

Vision Statement

The Junior League of Austin will strengthen our community through creative solutions to current and future challenges.

Contents

Introduction

Austin, the capital of Texas, is a paradox. Its culture is casual, yet sophisticated; comfortable, but bustling with energy; traditional, but also on the "cutting edge." It's a government town and a "green" town; a city of old hippies and high-tech. While other Texas cities may be known for their glamour and glitz, big oil money, or their history, Austin has always enjoyed a reputation as a laid-back kind of town. For years primarily a government and college town, Austin was known as the home of The University of Texas and state government. Austin's "quality of life" was shorthand for describing its gentle hills, many lakes, comfortable neighborhoods, outdoor activities, lively music scene, and well-educated population. Austinites still embrace the offbeat, remain environmentally attuned, and pursue what is "cool" like residents in no other Texas city. Some people say that Austin just isn't like the rest of Texas—but, don't be fooled; while Austinites may march to the beat of their own upbeat drummer, they are fiercely proud to be part of the Lone Star State and wouldn't have it any other way!!

Thanks and Credits

Central Market
Cornerstone
Breed & Co.
Feather Your Nest
The Menagerie
Neena's
Personally Yours
Pottery Barn
Burt Secord
Tina & Jon Kemmerer
Freddie & Lisa Fletcher
Lady Bird Johnson Wildflower Center
The University of Texas
    Sports Information Department
Austin Convention and Visitors Bureau

Chefs:
    Jeff Blank
    Patrick Dixson
    David Garrido
    Dan Haverty
    Tim Kartiganer
    Charles Mayes
    Jay Moore
    Peter O'Brien
    Mary Perna
    Roberto Santibañez
    Alma Thomas
    Kevin Williamson

Food Photography:
    David Grimes
    Jennifer Lindberg, assistant
    Will Phillips, assistant

Scenery Photography:
    Matthew Mahon

Layout/Design:
    Jennifer Taylor

Food Stylists:
    Laura Kooris
    Claire Hamilton, assistant

Other Photos:
    Richard Reynolds—photos of
        wildflowers and the
        Johnson City Courthouse
    Charla Wood—photo of chefs
    Paul Bardagjy—photo of
        Paramount Theatre
    Jim Sigmun—photo of
        University of Texas helmets
    Bob Daemmrich—photo of
        Ballet Folklorico
    Jim Winn Photography—
        cinematography photo
    Kraft Foods
    Willie Nelson

The Junior League of Austin

Austin Entertains

Cookbook Development Committee

Dinah Barksdale
Chair

Leslie Timmerman
Committee Assistant

Christine Malvezzi
Layout/Design Chair

Hayley Hughes
Recipe Chair

Annette Ramey-Graf
Sidebars Co-Chair

Kelly Barnhill
Sidebars Co-Chair

Sheri Krause
Parties Chair

Sharon Morris
Sustaining Advisor

Alison Campbell
Sustaining Advisor

Jan Bashur
Financial Development Vice President 1999–2000

Cookbook Marketing Team

Dinah Barksdale

Tamra Beasley

Elaine Brown

Cathy Cour

Molly Elder

Emily Forman

Donna Smith

Lee Wilpon

Lanette Smith
Financial Development Vice President 2000–2001

The Junior League of Austin

League Leadership

MariBen Ramsey
President 2000–2001

Nancy Edsel
President 1999–2000

Nancy Prideaux
President 1998–1999

A Christmas *Affair*

the Ultimate Fund-Raiser

Each November before Thanksgiving, The Junior League of Austin proudly presents its A Christmas Affair fund-raiser, which has kicked off the holiday season in the capital city for more than a quarter of a century. This nationally renowned holiday marketplace showcases more than 150 merchants from around the country. Coupled with special events and festive parties, A Christmas Affair attracts more than 30,000 visitors during the five-day event. Through the success of this holiday tradition, The Junior League of Austin has returned millions of dollars to Central Texas by funding programs and projects for hundreds of nonprofit organizations.

A Christmas Affair always begins with an evening of elegant private shopping. What better way could there be to start the evening than with a cocktail and hors d'oeuvre pre-party with friends?

Beverage

Christmas Cosmopolitan

Appetizers

Marinated Roasted Peppers with
  Red Onions on Garlic Pita Toasts
Baked Artichoke Dip
Sun-Dried Tomato Torta
Cocktail Beef Wellingtons
Asparagus Phyllo Roll-Ups
Stone Crab Claws with Lemon Mayonnaise
  (pictured at right)
Grilled Manhattan Shrimp
Seafood Tarts

Marinated Roasted Peppers with Red Onions on Garlic Pita Toasts

Garlic Pita Toasts
1/2 cup (1 stick) butter, softened
4 large garlic cloves, minced
1 tablespoon chopped fresh flat-leaf parsley or basil
1/2 teaspoon dried oregano
Freshly ground pepper to taste
3 large pita rounds
1/2 cup freshly grated Parmesan cheese

Roasted Red Pepper Topping and Assembly
4 red bell peppers, roasted, peeled, seeded, julienned
4 garlic cloves, minced
Freshly ground pepper to taste
1/4 cup olive oil
1/3 cup kalamata olives, slivered
1 small red onion
2 tablespoons drained capers
2 tablespoons chopped fresh basil
2 tablespoons balsamic vinegar
1/2 cup freshly grated Parmigiano-Reggiano cheese

For the toasts, combine the butter, garlic, parsley, oregano and pepper in a bowl and mix well. Cut each pita round into halves to form 2 pockets. Split the pockets into halves. Spread a thin layer of the butter mixture on the cut side of each half. Sprinkle with the cheese. Cut each half into 2 to 4 wedges. Arrange the wedges on a baking sheet. Chill, covered with plastic wrap, for up to 2 days.

For the topping, combine the roasted peppers and garlic in a bowl and toss to mix. Sprinkle with pepper. Drizzle with the olive oil. Stir in the olives. Let stand, covered with plastic wrap, at room temperature for several hours to allow the flavors to meld, stirring occasionally.

Slice the onion into halves through the stem end. Cut each half into very thin wedges. Separate the wedges. Combine the onion and capers with the roasted pepper mixture 1 to 2 hours before serving and mix well.

To assemble, stir the basil and balsamic vinegar into the roasted pepper mixture. Broil the toasts for 2 minutes or until golden brown and bubbly. Arrange the toasts on a serving platter. Spoon some of the roasted pepper topping on each toast. Sprinkle with the cheese and freshly ground pepper. Serve immediately.

Serves 8 to 12

Baked Artichoke Dip

Aïoli Sauce

1 egg yolk or equivalent amount of egg substitute
2 teaspoons fresh lemon juice
1 teaspoon minced garlic
$1/4$ teaspoon Dijon mustard
$1/4$ teaspoon kosher salt
$1/4$ teaspoon chopped fresh parsley
White pepper to taste
$3/4$ cup extra-virgin olive oil

Artichoke Dip

$1/4$ cup chopped onion
1 teaspoon extra-virgin olive oil
1 (14-ounce) can artichoke hearts, drained
$1/3$ cup freshly grated Parmesan cheese
2 tablespoons freshly grated asiago cheese
2 tablespoons freshly grated Romano cheese
$1/4$ teaspoon minced garlic
$1/4$ teaspoon white pepper
$1/4$ teaspoon kosher salt
$1/3$ cup freshly grated Parmesan cheese
2 teaspoons finely minced fresh basil

For the sauce, combine the egg yolk, lemon juice, garlic, Dijon mustard, kosher salt, parsley and white pepper in a blender or food processor. Process until blended. Add the olive oil gradually, processing constantly until of a mayonnaise consistency.

For the dip, sauté the onion in the olive oil in a medium skillet until tender. Remove from heat. Place the artichokes in a large bowl, breaking up the artichokes slightly. Add the sauce, $1/3$ cup Parmesan cheese, asiago cheese, Romano cheese, garlic, white pepper and kosher salt and mix gently.

Spoon the artichoke mixture into a 1-quart baking dish. Sprinkle with $1/3$ cup Parmesan cheese. Bake at 450 degrees for 8 to 10 minutes or until golden brown. Cool slightly. Sprinkle with the basil. Serve with chips and/or assorted party crackers.

Serves 6 to 8

Christmas Cosmopolitan

Place 2 martini glasses in the freezer for 10 minutes or longer. Fill a cocktail shaker halfway with ice. Add $3^1/2$ ounces lemon-scented vodka, 2 tablespoons fresh lime juice, 2 ounces Cointreau and 1 tablespoon fresh cranberry juice; cover. Shake vigorously for 30 seconds. Strain evenly into the chilled glasses. Top with lime zest. Serves 2.

Crudités are bite-size pieces of fresh vegetables or fruits arranged on a tray and served as an appetizer, usually with some sort of cold sauce. Crudités always make a wonderful addition to any cocktail party. They provide not only a healthy alternative for your guests, but the vibrant colors of the assorted fresh vegetables and fruits can be a beautiful focal point for your table. Be sure that you cut each vegetable into bite-size pieces. To enhance both the flavor and the color of the green vegetables in your arrangement, we suggest blanching them to the al dente stage. Most vegetables take two to three minutes, depending on their sizes and diameters. Some of our favorite vegetables to use include: small artichokes, asparagus, assorted bell peppers (cut into rings or strips), baby carrots, brussels sprouts, cauliflower, cherry tomatoes, fennel, haricots verts, radishes, yellow squash, and zucchini. Get creative, and serve your favorite dipping sauce in a hollowed-out cabbage, pepper, or squash.

Sun-Dried Tomato Torta

$3/4$ cup sun-dried tomatoes
$1^1/2$ cups fresh basil leaves
3 garlic cloves, minced
$2/3$ cup pine nuts
3 tablespoons butter, softened
16 ounces cream cheese, softened, chopped
4 ounces feta cheese, crumbled
4 ounces goat cheese, crumbled
$1/2$ cup (1 stick) butter, softened
1 (7-ounce) jar roasted red bell peppers, drained, chopped
1 cup sliced kalamata olives

Rehydrate the sun-dried tomatoes in enough boiling water to cover in a heatproof bowl for 20 minutes; drain. Process the sun-dried tomatoes, basil and garlic in a food processor until finely chopped.

Line 2 small loaf pans with plastic wrap. Process $1/4$ cup of the pine nuts and 3 tablespoons butter in a food processor until the pine nuts are ground. Stir in the remaining pine nuts. Combine the cream cheese, feta cheese, goat cheese and $1/2$ cup butter in a food processor. Process until smooth.

Layer $1/3$ of the cream cheese mixture, sun-dried tomato mixture, $1/2$ of the remaining cream cheese mixture, roasted bell peppers and remaining cream cheese mixture in the prepared loaf pans. Top with the olives. Chill, covered with plastic wrap, for 8 to 10 hours. Serve with sliced French bread or assorted party crackers.

Serves 20 to 25

Cocktail Beef Wellingtons

Béarnaise Sauce
3 egg yolks or equivalent amount of egg substitute
3 tablespoons lemon juice
$1/8$ teaspoon salt
$1/2$ cup (1 stick) butter, melted
1 teaspoon dried tarragon

Beef Wellingtons
6 tablespoons olive oil
3 tablespoons red wine vinegar
2 tablespoons sugar
1 teaspoon Dijon mustard
1 teaspoon each salt and pepper
1 pound beef tenderloin, cut into bite-size pieces
3 cups chopped fresh mushrooms
$1/4$ cup chopped shallots
2 tablespoons butter
Salt and pepper to taste
20 sheets frozen phyllo pastry, thawed
6 tablespoons butter, melted

For the sauce, combine the egg yolks, lemon juice and salt in a blender. Process until blended. Add the butter gradually, processing constantly until thickened. Pour into a bowl. Whisk in the tarragon.

For the Wellingtons, whisk the olive oil, wine vinegar, sugar, Dijon mustard, salt and pepper in a bowl. Add the beef and toss to coat. Marinate, covered, in the refrigerator for 4 to 6 hours, stirring occasionally; drain.

Sauté the mushrooms and shallots in 2 tablespoons butter in a skillet for 5 minutes. Season with salt and pepper. Cool to room temperature. Unroll the pastry and cover with waxed paper topped with a damp tea towel to prevent it from drying out, removing 2 sheets at a time. Brush 1 sheet with some of the melted butter. Stack with another sheet and brush with the melted butter. Cut the stack lengthwise into four 3-inch strips. Place 1 piece of the beef and 1 teaspoon of the mushroom mixture on the end of each strip. Fold the corner over to the opposite edge to cover the filling, forming a triangle. Continue folding like a flag. Arrange seam side down on a greased baking sheet. Repeat the process with the remaining pastry, melted butter, beef and mushroom mixture. Bake at 375 degrees for 10 minutes or until light brown. Serve with the sauce.

Makes 40

Asparagus Phyllo Roll-Ups

10 sheets frozen phyllo pastry, thawed
$^1/_4$ cup ($^1/_2$ stick) butter, melted
$^1/_3$ to $^2/_3$ cup freshly grated Parmesan cheese
30 fresh asparagus spears, blanched
1 roasted red bell pepper, skins removed, cut into 30 strips
4 ounces bleu cheese, crumbled

Unroll the pastry and cover with waxed paper topped with a damp tea towel to prevent it from drying out. Remove 1 sheet of the phyllo at a time. Brush with some of the butter and sprinkle with 1 to 2 tablespoons of the Parmesan cheese. Layer with another sheet of pastry and brush with butter.

Cut the stack horizontally into 3 strips. Cut each strip into halves. Arrange 1 asparagus spear, 1 bell pepper strip and 1 teaspoon of the bleu cheese at the short end of the pastry and roll to enclose the filling. Arrange on a baking sheet sprayed with nonstick cooking spray. Repeat the process with the remaining ingredients. Bake at 375 degrees for 15 minutes or until brown.

Makes 30 roll-ups

Stone Crab Claws with Lemon Mayonnaise

2 cups mayonnaise
$^1/_4$ cup each Dijon mustard and lemon juice
2 tablespoons Worcestershire sauce
1 tablespoon Tabasco sauce
1 teaspoon grated lemon zest
$^1/_8$ teaspoon cayenne pepper
Salt and black pepper to taste
2 tablespoons grated lemon zest
Cayenne pepper to taste
40 stone crab claws, steamed
Sprigs of dill

Combine the mayonnaise, Dijon mustard, lemon juice, Worcestershire sauce, Tabasco sauce, 1 teaspoon lemon zest, $^1/_8$ teaspoon cayenne pepper, salt and black pepper in a bowl and mix well. Chill, covered, for 2 days to allow the flavors to meld. Spoon the lemon mayonnaise into a bowl. Sprinkle with 2 tablespoons lemon zest and cayenne pepper to taste and garnish with fresh dill. Arrange the stone crabs on a platter. Serve with the lemon mayonnaise.

Makes 40 pieces

Photograph for this recipe is on page 14.

Grilled Manhattan Shrimp

5 pounds jumbo shrimp
1 bunch cilantro, trimmed
5 to 6 serrano chiles, seeded
5 to 6 garlic cloves
1 cup lime juice
$1/2$ teaspoon brown sugar
Salt and pepper to taste
$2^1/4$ cups olive oil

Peel and devein the shrimp, leaving the tails intact. Place in a bowl. Process the cilantro, serrano chiles and garlic in a food processor or blender until finely chopped. Add the lime juice, brown sugar, salt and pepper. Add 2 cups of the olive oil gradually, processing constantly until emulsified.

Pour the olive oil mixture over the shrimp, turning to coat. Marinate, covered, in the refrigerator for 20 to 60 minutes, stirring occasionally; drain. Thread the shrimp on skewers and brush with the remaining $1/4$ cup olive oil. Grill over hot coals for 3 to 4 minutes per side or until the shrimp turn pink.

Serves 12 to 15

Seafood Tarts

1 loaf very thin white bread
$1/2$ cup (1 stick) butter, melted
1 cup mayonnaise
3 ounces each crab meat and deveined peeled cooked shrimp
$1/3$ cup each freshly grated Parmesan cheese and shredded Swiss cheese
$1/3$ cup chopped onion
$1/2$ teaspoon Worcestershire sauce
2 to 3 drops of Tabasco sauce
Paprika to taste

Trim the crusts from the bread and flatten slightly with a rolling pin. Cut rounds from the centers of each slice with a 3-inch round cutter. Dip each round into the butter. Press the rounds into miniature muffin cups. Bake at 400 degrees for 10 minutes.

Combine the mayonnaise, crab meat, shrimp, Parmesan cheese, Swiss cheese, onion, Worcestershire sauce and Tabasco sauce in a food processor. Pulse slightly or just until mixed. Spoon into the prepared muffin cups. Sprinkle with paprika. Bake for 10 minutes. Serve immediately.

Makes 25 tarts

Over the *River* and through the *Hills*

Central Texas holidays are a visual delight. Country courthouses are decked in glowing lights. Luminarias, small paper bags illuminated by candles, line walkways and streets. In Austin, the lighting of the beautiful Zilker Park Christmas Tree of lights heralds the holiday season. No visit to this Austin landmark is complete without a dizzying twirl under the canopy of lights. The annual Trail of Lights offers a fantastical promenade through wintry Christmas scenes and high-tech laser light shows. O. Henry's "The Gift of the Magi," one of the most beloved holiday stories known the world over, was written in Austin. Learn more about O. Henry's life, and his time in Austin, when you visit the O. Henry Museum. Don't miss the Ballet Austin's annual *Nutcracker* with the Austin Symphony.

Menu

Savor the special foods that celebrate Austin traditions—from our families to yours.

Appetizers
Crostini with Herb Butter
Crab-Stuffed Cherry Tomatoes
Crab Cakes with Avocado Sauce
Bleu Cheesecake
Spicy Cayenne Toasts
Goat Cheese Croutons

Soups
Creamy Asparagus and Mushroom Soup
Tomato Soup

Salads
Mushrooms and Herbed Goat Cheese in Puff Pastry over
    Field Greens
Smoked Salmon Salad and Crème Fraîche

Entrées
Beef Tenderloin with Green Peppercorn Cognac Sauce
Crown Pork Roast with Wild Rice Stuffing
    (pictured at right)
Seafood Supreme

Side Dishes
Sesame Broccoli
Green Beans with Shallots and Red Pepper
Hudson's Corn Pudding

Bread
Sun-Dried Tomato Rolls

Desserts
Chocolate Peppermint Soufflés
Chocolate Chunk Hazelnut Cake with Raspberry Sauce
Truffle Cake
Easy Toffee

Crab Cakes with Avocado Sauce

1 each green, red and yellow bell pepper, finely chopped
4 scallions, chopped
1/4 cup chopped cilantro
16 ounces crab meat
1/2 teaspoon salt
1/2 teaspoon freshly ground pepper
1/2 teaspoon dried thyme
1/4 teaspoon Tabasco sauce
6 tablespoons mayonnaise
1 1/2 cups bread crumbs
Avocado Sauce (below)

Reserve half the bell peppers and half the scallions for the garnish. Combine the remaining bell peppers, remaining scallions, cilantro, crab meat, salt, pepper, thyme and Tabasco sauce in a bowl and mix gently. Stir in the mayonnaise. Add the bread crumbs and toss lightly.

Shape the mixture into 3-inch patties. Handle the mixture gently, as it should barely adhere. Sauté the crab cakes in a nonstick skillet over medium heat for 3 to 5 minutes or until golden brown on both sides.

Puddle some of the Avocado Sauce in the center of each serving plate. Arrange 1 crab cake on each plate. Sprinkle with the reserved bell peppers and reserved scallions. Serve immediately.

Serves 4 or 5

Avocado Sauce

1 medium ripe avocado, chopped
1/2 cup sour cream
1/4 cup chopped fresh cilantro
2 tablespoons lemon juice
1/8 teaspoon sugar
1/8 teaspoon salt
1/8 teaspoon pepper

Combine the avocado, sour cream, cilantro, lemon juice, sugar, salt and pepper in a food processor. Process until smooth. Chill, covered, until serving time.

Makes 1 cup

Bleu Cheesecake

2 tablespoons butter or margarine
1 cup crushed cheese wafers or cheese crackers
16 ounces cream cheese, softened
8 ounces bleu cheese, at room temperature
1 cup sour cream
3 eggs
1/4 cup flour
1/4 cup medium picante sauce
1/4 teaspoon salt
1/2 cup chopped green onions
1/2 cup chopped walnuts

Brush the bottom and side of a springform pan with the butter and coat with cracker crumbs. Beat the cream cheese, bleu cheese, sour cream, eggs, flour, picante sauce and salt in a mixing bowl until blended. Fold in the green onions. Spoon the cream cheese mixture into the prepared pan. Sprinkle with the walnuts. Bake at 325 degrees for 1 hour. Let stand until cool. Chill, covered, for 8 to 10 hours. Serve with assorted party crackers. May substitute pecans for the walnuts.

Serves 15 to 20

Creamy Tomato Soup

2 bunches scallions, chopped
1/2 cup (1 stick) butter
8 ripe tomatoes, chopped
1 cup dry white wine
1 tablespoon chopped fresh dill
4 cups milk
2 cups whipping cream
2 (8-ounce) cans tomato sauce
Salt and pepper to taste

Sauté the scallions in the butter in a saucepan until tender. Stir in the tomatoes, wine and dill. Cook for 15 minutes, stirring occasionally. Add the milk, whipping cream, tomato sauce, salt and pepper and mix well. Simmer for 1 hour, stirring occasionally. Ladle into soup bowls.

Serves 6 to 8

Spicy Cayenne Toasts

Cut 1 French bread baguette into 1/4-inch slices. Arrange the slices in a single layer on a baking sheet. Combine 1/2 cup olive oil, 2 teaspoons cayenne pepper, 1 1/2 teaspoons garlic powder, 1 teaspoon salt, 1 teaspoon sugar and 1/2 teaspoon paprika in a jar with a tight-fitting lid; cover. Shake to mix. Brush 1 side of each bread slice lightly with the olive oil mixture. Bake at 200 degrees for 1 hour or until crisp. Remove to a wire rack to cool. You may prepare in advance and store, covered, in the freezer. Makes 3 dozen.

Goat Cheese Croutons

Brush both sides of eight ¹/₂-inch-thick slices of French or Italian bread with olive oil and sprinkle with salt and freshly ground pepper. Arrange the slices in a single layer on a baking sheet. Bake at 350 degrees for 4 minutes or until light brown, turning once. Top each crouton with a ¹/₄-inch-thick slice of goat cheese. Sprinkle with 1 tablespoon minced fresh thyme, salt and freshly ground pepper. Serves 8.

Asparagus and Mushroom Soup

Soup

2 tablespoons olive oil
10 ounces shiitake mushrooms, stems removed, thinly sliced
¹/₄ teaspoon salt
¹/₄ teaspoon freshly ground pepper
1¹/₂ tablespoons olive oil
1 large onion, chopped
1 quart water
1 quart canned reduced-sodium chicken broth or homemade chicken stock
¹/₃ cup long grain rice
2 teaspoons salt
2 pounds asparagus, trimmed, cut into 1-inch slices

Garnish

16 (¹/₂-inch) baguette slices
3 tablespoons olive oil
4 ounces Gruyère cheese, shredded

For the soup, heat 2 tablespoons olive oil in a large saucepan over medium-high heat until hot. Add the mushrooms, ¹/₄ teaspoon salt and pepper. Cook for 5 minutes or until the mushrooms are golden brown, stirring occasionally. Remove the mushrooms with a slotted spoon to a bowl, reserving the pan drippings. Reduce the heat to medium-low.

Add 1¹/₂ tablespoons olive oil to the reserved pan drippings. Stir in the onion. Cook for 5 minutes or until tender, stirring occasionally. Stir in the water, broth, rice and 2 teaspoons salt. Bring to a boil. Boil for 10 minutes, stirring occasionally. Stir in the asparagus.

Cook for 5 minutes longer or until the asparagus is tender, stirring occasionally. Process the soup in a blender or food processor until smooth. Return the soup to the saucepan. Stir in the mushrooms. Cook just until heated through. Remove from heat. Cover to keep warm.

For the garnish, brush both sides of the bread slices with 3 tablespoons olive oil. Arrange the slices in a single layer on a baking sheet. Broil for 2 minutes or until brown; turn. Sprinkle with the cheese. Broil for 2 minutes longer or until the cheese melts.

Reheat the soup if necessary. Ladle into soup bowls. Sprinkle with additional Gruyère cheese. Serve with the cheese-topped bread slices. You may substitute 8 ounces sliced white mushrooms with stems for the shiitake mushrooms.

Serves 8

Mushrooms and Herbed Goat Cheese in Puff Pastry over Field Greens

Sherry Vinaigrette

1/2 cup olive oil
2 tablespoons sherry vinegar
1 tablespoon sugar
2 teaspoons chopped fresh basil
2 teaspoons Dijon mustard
1 teaspoon salt

Salad

1 pound portobello mushroom caps, cut into 1/4-inch slices
1 pound oyster mushrooms, stemmed, coarsely chopped
2 tablespoons olive oil
4 shallots, finely chopped
2 garlic cloves, minced
2 tablespoons chopped fresh herbs, such as flat-leaf parsley, chives, oregano or rosemary
8 puff pastry shells
4 ounces goat cheese, crumbled
Mixed field greens, trimmed, torn

For the vinaigrette, whisk the olive oil, sherry vinegar, sugar, basil, Dijon mustard and salt in a bowl until mixed.

For the salad, sauté the mushrooms in the olive oil in a skillet over high heat just until seared on all sides. Add the shallots and garlic. Sauté until the mushrooms are tender. Remove from heat. Stir in the fresh herbs.

Arrange the pastry shells on a baking sheet. Reserve 1/4 cup of the goat cheese. Divide the remaining goat cheese evenly among the pastry shells. Spoon the mushroom mixture over the goat cheese. Sprinkle with the reserved goat cheese. Bake at 350 degrees for 5 minutes or until the cheese melts and the mushroom mixture is heated through.

Toss the greens with the vinaigrette in a bowl until coated and spoon evenly onto 8 serving plates. Arrange 1 mushroom-filled pastry shell on each plate. Serve immediately.

Serves 8

Puff pastry is a delicate French pastry made by infusing pats of chilled butter between layers of a very thin pastry, rolling it out, folding it into thirds, and repeating the process many times. Luckily, you can usually buy this product at your local market—we'll gladly take this route! Puff pastry has the reputation of being hard to handle, but put your fears aside and get out your rolling pin. A product this versatile should be a staple in every kitchen. Follow the thawing directions on the package, then roll the puff pastry on a lightly floured surface. It can be used to package anything from cheese (Brie cheese is a great choice), to meat, as in Beef Wellington; just make sure you seal the edges well with beaten egg. Brushing the outer surface of your completed parcel with an egg wash will also give it a delicate and attractive shine. You can also cut strips of puff pastry dough and bake them to use for Napoleon layers. To make a salad really festive, make puff pastry croutons. Use small cookie cutters to form desired shapes, brush with egg wash, and sprinkle with grated Parmesan cheese, then bake. The possibilities are endless—just use your imagination.

Crab-Stuffed Cherry Tomatoes

Scoop the pulp from 3 dozen cherry tomatoes, discarding the pulp. Invert the tomatoes onto paper towels to drain. Toss 1 cup shredded crab meat and 1/4 cup fresh lime juice in a bowl. Marinate, covered, in the refrigerator for 1 hour; drain. Combine with 3 ounces softened cream cheese, 1/4 cup cream, 2 tablespoons mayonnaise, 1 tablespoon minced onion, 1 teaspoon dried dill, 1 teaspoon Worcestershire sauce, 1/2 teaspoon minced garlic, 2 drops of Tabasco sauce and salt to taste. Stuff the drained tomatoes with the crab meat filling. Chill until serving time. Makes 3 dozen.

Smoked Salmon Salad with Crème Fraîche

Crème Fraîche
  1 cup heavy cream
  1 cup sour cream

Salad
  1 pound smoked salmon, chopped
  1 small red onion, minced
  1/4 cup drained capers
  1 1/2 tablespoons chopped fresh thyme,
     or 3/4 teaspoon dried thyme
  1 teaspoon freshly ground pepper
  1/2 cup rice vinegar
  1/2 cup extra-virgin olive oil
  Salt to taste
  12 cups assorted baby lettuces
  1/4 cup caviar, preferably sevruga

For the crème fraîche, combine the heavy cream and sour cream in a 1-pint glass jar and stir to mix. Let stand, uncovered, at room temperature for 2 to 4 hours or until thickened. Chill, covered, for 6 hours or for up to 10 days before serving.

For the salad, combine the salmon, onion, capers, thyme and pepper in a bowl and mix gently. Drizzle with the rice vinegar and olive oil and toss to mix. Season with salt. Spoon the salmon mixture onto 8 lettuce-lined salad plates. Top each serving with 2 tablespoons of the crème fraîche, reserving the remaining crème fraîche for another recipe. Sprinkle with the caviar. Serve immediately with toast points or crusty French bread.

Serves 8

Beef Tenderloin with Green Peppercorn Cognac Sauce

Beef Tenderloin
1 (3-pound) beef tenderloin
Beau Monde seasoning to taste
Lemon pepper to taste
2 cups soy sauce

Green Peppercorn Cognac Sauce
1 cup chicken broth
1 cup beef broth
3 tablespoons chopped shallots
2 tablespoons green peppercorns, crushed
1 tablespoon butter
$1/2$ cup dry red wine vinegar
$2^1/2$ tablespoons Cognac
2 cups whipping cream
2 tablespoons prepared horseradish

For the tenderloin, sprinkle the entire surface of the tenderloin with Beau Monde seasoning and lemon pepper. Pour the soy sauce over the tenderloin in a shallow dish, turning to coat. Marinate, covered, in the refrigerator for 2 hours, turning every 30 minutes; drain.

Arrange the tenderloin on a rack in a baking pan. Bake at 350 degrees for 30 minutes or until a meat thermometer registers 110 to 115 degrees for rare. Remove to a serving platter. Let stand for several minutes before carving.

For the sauce, combine the chicken broth and beef broth in a saucepan and mix well. Bring to a boil. Boil for 15 minutes or until reduced to $1/2$ cup, stirring occasionally. Remove from heat.

Sauté the shallots and peppercorns in the butter in a saucepan over medium heat for 5 minutes or until the shallots are golden brown. Increase the heat to high. Add the wine vinegar and Cognac and mix well. Bring to a boil.

Boil for 4 minutes or until reduced to $1/4$ cup, stirring frequently. Stir in the reduced broth and whipping cream. Bring to a boil. Boil for 5 minutes or until thickened, stirring frequently. Remove from heat. Stir in the horseradish. Serve with the tenderloin.

Serves 6

Crown Pork Roast with Wild Rice Stuffing

Wild Rice Stuffing

4 cups cooked wild rice
2 cups dried cranberries, coarsely
    chopped, rehydrated
$1/2$ cup (1 stick) butter
$3^1/2$ tablespoons sugar
1 garlic clove, finely minced

1 teaspoon salt
$1/2$ teaspoon dried marjoram
$1/2$ teaspoon mace
$1/2$ teaspoon dried thyme
$1/2$ teaspoon dried dill
$1/4$ teaspoon pepper

Crown Pork Roast

1 crown pork roast (18 chops),
    trimmed

Mustard Sauce and Assembly

$1/4$ cup pork roast pan drippings or
    butter
$1/4$ cup flour
1 cup dry white wine
$1/2$ cup chicken broth
$1/2$ cup heavy cream

3 tablespoons Dijon mustard
1 teaspoon dry mustard
Salt and pepper to taste
Orange or peach slices
Endive
Brussels sprouts

For the stuffing, combine the wild rice, cranberries, butter, sugar, garlic, salt, marjoram, mace, thyme, dill and pepper in a saucepan and mix well. Cook over medium-low heat until heated through, stirring occasionally. Let stand until cool.

For the pork, protect the ends of the bones by covering with foil to prevent burning. Place the roast on a rack lined with foil in a roasting pan. Roast at 350 degrees for 20 minutes per pound. Mound the stuffing in the crown 1 hour before the end of the roasting process, covering with foil if necessary to prevent overbrowning. Extra stuffing may be baked, covered, for 30 minutes.

For the sauce, combine the pan drippings and flour in a saucepan and mix well. Cook over low heat for 3 minutes, stirring constantly. Stir in the wine. Cook for 3 minutes or until thickened, stirring constantly. Add the broth and heavy cream and mix well. Cook for 5 minutes, stirring frequently. Stir in the Dijon mustard, dry mustard, salt and pepper.

To assemble, place the roast on a serving platter. Arrange endive, brussels sprouts and assorted fruits around the roast. Serve with the sauce.

Serves 8 to 10

Photograph for this recipe is on page 24.

Seafood Supreme

3/4 cup (1¹/2 sticks) butter
9 tablespoons flour
1 teaspoon salt
¹/8 teaspoon pepper
¹/8 teaspoon garlic powder
2 cups milk
1 cup cream
3 egg yolks, lightly beaten
1 cup dry white wine
1 cup shredded Swiss cheese
2 pounds shrimp, cooked, peeled, deveined
2 pounds scallops, cooked
1¹/2 pounds lobster meat, cooked
Bread crumbs to taste
Shredded Swiss cheese to taste

Heat the butter in a saucepan until melted. Stir in the flour, salt, pepper and garlic powder. Cook until bubbly, stirring constantly. Add the milk and cream gradually, stirring constantly until blended. Cook over low heat until thick and smooth, stirring constantly. Stir 6 tablespoons of the hot sauce into the egg yolks. Stir the egg yolks into the hot mixture.

Cook over low heat for 5 minutes, stirring frequently. Add the wine and 1 cup Swiss cheese and mix well. Cook until blended, stirring constantly. Stir in the shrimp, scallops and lobster meat. Spoon into a baking dish. Sprinkle with bread crumbs and Swiss cheese to taste. Bake at 350 degrees for 15 minutes.

Serves 6 to 8

Crostini with Herb Butter

Cut 1 small French bread baguette diagonally into ¹/4-inch-thick slices. Arrange the slices in a single layer on a baking sheet. Mix ¹/4 cup melted unsalted butter, 2 tablespoons minced fresh parsley, 2 tablespoons minced fresh basil and 1 teaspoon finely minced garlic in a bowl. Season with salt and pepper. Brush the bread slices with the butter mixture. Bake at 350 degrees for 8 to 10 minutes or until golden brown and crisp. Makes 2 to 3 dozen.

Sesame Broccoli

$1/4$ cup sesame seeds, toasted
$1/4$ cup sake
3 tablespoons soy sauce
2 teaspoons honey
2 teaspoons sesame oil
Florets of 1 bunch broccoli, blanched
1 roasted red bell pepper, skin removed, chopped

Whisk the sesame seeds, sake, soy sauce, honey and sesame oil in a bowl. Add the broccoli and bell pepper and toss gently to coat. Serve immediately. Prepare the sauce in advance and toss with the broccoli just before serving.

Serves 4

Green Beans with Shallots and Red Pepper

2 pounds fresh green beans, trimmed
3 large shallots, finely chopped
1 large red bell pepper, julienned
$1/3$ cup butter
1 teaspoon kosher salt
Pepper to taste

Blanch the beans in boiling water in a saucepan for 3 to 4 minutes or until of the desired degree of crispness; drain. Sauté the shallots and bell pepper in the butter in a skillet for 4 to 5 minutes or until tender. Stir in the beans, salt and pepper. Cook just until heated through, stirring frequently. Spoon into a serving bowl. Serve immediately.

Serves 6

Hudson's Corn Pudding

1 green bell pepper, chopped
1 red bell pepper, chopped
1 Anaheim chile, chopped
$1^1/_2$ cups flour
$^1/_2$ cup sugar
5 tablespoons baking powder
$^3/_4$ tablespoon salt
$1^1/_2$ teaspoons cayenne pepper
10 eggs
1 cup whipping cream
$^3/_4$ cup ($1^1/_2$ sticks) butter, melted
2 (8-ounce) cans cream-style corn
2 pounds fresh or frozen whole kernel corn

Combine the bell peppers and Anaheim chile in a bowl and mix well. Combine the flour, sugar, baking powder, salt and cayenne pepper in a bowl and mix well.

Whisk the eggs lightly in a bowl. Add the whipping cream, butter and cream-style corn and whisk until mixed. Add the corn mixture gradually to the flour mixture, stirring constantly until mixed. Stir in the bell pepper mixture and whole kernel corn. Spoon into a greased and floured 9×13-inch baking pan. Bake at 375 degrees for 40 to 45 minutes or until set and light brown.

Chefs Jeff Blank and Jay Moore of Hudson's-on-the-Bend contributed this recipe.

Serves 16 to 20

Sun-Dried Tomato Rolls

2 ounces sun-dried tomatoes
1 medium tomato
6 cups bread flour
$1/4$ cup sugar
Kosher salt to taste
1 envelope dry yeast
$3/4$ cup milk, heated
4 eggs
$1/2$ cup (1 stick) butter, softened
2 tablespoons olive oil
$1/4$ teaspoon minced garlic

Pour enough hot water to cover the sun-dried tomatoes in a heatproof bowl. Let stand for 2 to 3 hours or until soft. Drain and coarsely chop the sun-dried tomatoes.

Immerse the tomato in boiling water in a saucepan until the peel begins to split. Remove the tomato with a slotted spoon. Let stand until cool. Remove the peel. Process the tomato in a blender until puréed.

Sift the bread flour, sugar and kosher salt into a bowl and mix well. Combine the tomato purée, yeast and milk in a large mixing bowl and mix well. Add the bread flour mixture. Beat at low speed with a mixer with a dough hook attachment until smooth. Add the eggs 1 at a time, beating well after each addition. Knead at medium speed until elastic. Add the butter. Beat until blended. Add the sun-dried tomatoes. Beat until the dough clings to the hook and the sides of the bowl are clean. The dough will be smooth and elastic.

Place the dough in a greased bowl, turning to coat the surface. Let rise, covered, until doubled in bulk. Punch the dough down. Chill, covered, in the refrigerator. Shape the dough into 24 balls. Arrange the balls in 24 lightly greased muffin cups. Sprinkle lightly with kosher salt. Slash the top of each ball with a sharp knife. Let rise, covered, in a warm place until doubled in bulk.

Bake at 400 degrees for 10 to 12 minutes or until light brown. Brush the tops with a mixture of the olive oil and garlic. Remove to a wire rack to cool.

Makes 2 dozen rolls

Chocolate Peppermint Soufflés

Chocolate Peppermint Sauce

1 cup whipping cream
1 cup crushed peppermint candy
    canes or other hard peppermint
    candies

$1/4$ cup water
6 ounces semisweet chocolate,
    chopped

Chocolate Soufflés

Sugar to taste
3 tablespoons unsalted butter
3 tablespoons flour
1 cup 2% milk
$1/4$ teaspoon salt
6 ounces semisweet chocolate,
    chopped
$2/3$ cup sugar

$1/2$ cup water
1 teaspoon vanilla extract
5 egg yolks, beaten
6 egg whites
$1/4$ teaspoon cream of tartar
$1/3$ cup crushed peppermint candy
    canes or other hard peppermint
    candies

For the sauce, combine the whipping cream, candy and water in a heavy saucepan. Cook over medium heat until the candy melts, stirring frequently. Remove from heat. Add the chocolate, stirring until blended. Serve warm or at room temperature. You may prepare up to 1 day in advance. Store, covered, in the refrigerator. Reheat over low heat.

For the soufflés, butter eight $1^1/4$-cup soufflé dishes or custard cups. Sprinkle with sugar to taste. Arrange the dishes on a large baking sheet. Heat 3 tablespoons butter in a saucepan over medium heat until melted. Whisk in the flour. Cook for 2 minutes or until the mixture is bubbly and smooth, whisking constantly. Increase the heat to medium-high. Add the 2% milk gradually, whisking constantly.

Cook for 1 minute or until the mixture comes to a boil and is thick and smooth, whisking constantly. Whisk in the salt. Remove from heat. Add the chocolate and whisk until blended. Whisk in $1/3$ cup of the sugar, water and vanilla. Let stand for 25 minutes or until room temperature.

Whisk the egg yolks into the chocolate mixture. Beat the egg whites and cream of tartar in a mixing bowl until soft peaks form. Add the remaining $1/3$ cup sugar gradually, beating constantly until stiff and glossy. Fold $1/4$ of the beaten egg whites into the chocolate mixture. Fold the chocolate mixture into the remaining beaten egg whites in 3 additions. Spoon into the prepared dishes. Sprinkle with the candy. You may prepare to this point up to 3 days in advance, wrap in foil and freeze. Remove foil and bake; do not thaw.

Bake the soufflés at 400 degrees for 30 minutes or until puffed and almost firm to the touch but still soft in the center. Bake frozen soufflés for 40 minutes. Serve immediately with the sauce.

Serves 8

Chocolate Chunk Hazelnut Cake with Raspberry Sauce

Raspberry Sauce
2 cups fresh raspberries
3 tablespoons superfine sugar
4 teaspoons raspberry liqueur

Cake
9 ounces semisweet chocolate, chopped
2 tablespoons unseasoned bread crumbs
1 cup ground hazelnuts
$1/2$ teaspoon baking powder
1 cup (2 sticks) unsalted butter, softened
1 cup sugar
7 egg yolks
2 tablespoons amaretto
7 egg whites
Confectioners' sugar
1 cup whipping cream
$1/2$ teaspoon sugar

For the sauce, process the raspberries, sugar and liqueur in a blender or food processor until puréed; strain. Chill, covered, until serving time.

For the cake, coat the side and bottom of a 10-inch springform pan with butter. Line the bottom with waxed paper. Coat the waxed paper with butter and dust the side and bottom of the pan with flour. Combine the chocolate, bread crumbs, hazelnuts and baking powder in a bowl and mix well.

Beat the butter in a mixing bowl until creamy, scraping the bowl occasionally. Add 1 cup sugar. Beat until blended. Add the egg yolks 1 at a time, beating well after each addition. Beat in the amaretto. Fold in the chocolate mixture.

Beat the egg whites in a mixing bowl until soft peaks form. Lighten the chocolate mixture by folding in $1/4$ of the egg whites. Fold the remaining egg whites into the chocolate mixture until combined. Spoon the batter into the prepared pan. Place the pan on the lowest oven rack. Bake at 350 degrees for 50 to 60 minutes or until a wooden pick inserted in the center comes out clean. Cool in the pan on a wire rack. The cake will immediately shrink from the side of the pan and cracks will appear on the top.

Invert the cake and loosen the edge of the waxed paper with a sharp knife, discarding the waxed paper. Invert onto a cake plate. Sift lightly with confectioners' sugar.

Beat the whipping cream and $1/2$ teaspoon sugar in a mixing bowl until soft peaks form. Cut the cake into thin slices. Swirl some of the sauce onto each dessert plate. Arrange a slice of the cake over the sauce. Top with the whipped cream. Garnish with additional fresh raspberries. Serve immediately.

Serves 10 to 12

Truffle Cake

8 ounces amaretti, crushed
$^1/_4$ to $^1/_2$ cup Grand Marnier or kirsch
16 ounces dark chocolate, chopped
$^1/_2$ cup (1 stick) unsalted butter, softened
2 egg yolks or equivalent amount of egg substitute
$2^1/_2$ cups whipping cream
Confectioners' sugar

Soak the cookie crumbs in the Grand Marnier in a bowl. Heat the chocolate in a double boiler over hot water until melted, stirring occasionally. Remove from heat. Add the butter, stirring until smooth.

Whisk the egg yolks in a bowl until blended. Stir a small amount of the chocolate mixture into the egg yolks. Stir the egg yolks into the chocolate mixture. Let stand until cool.

Beat the whipping cream in a mixing bowl until soft peaks form. Fold into the chocolate mixture. Layer the chocolate mixture and cookie mixture alternately in a greased 8-inch springform pan until all of the ingredients are used. Chill, covered, for several hours. Dust with confectioners' sugar before serving.

Serves 8 to 10

Easy Toffee

1 cup chopped almonds or pecans
1 cup sugar
$^3/_4$ cup ($1^1/_2$ sticks) butter
$^1/_2$ teaspoon salt
2 teaspoons vanilla extract
1 cup (6 ounces) chocolate chips

Spread the almonds in a single layer on a buttered baking sheet. Combine the sugar, butter and salt in a saucepan. Cook until blended and the color of peanut butter, stirring constantly. Remove from heat. Stir in the vanilla.

Drizzle the syrup over the almonds. Sprinkle with the chocolate chips and spread evenly over the top as the chocolate chips soften. Let stand until firm. Break into 2 dozen pieces.

Makes 2 dozen

Hot chocolate is a great way to take the chill off cool winter nights. Hot chocolate is sure to warm everyone's heart, young and old alike. Be sure to garnish with lots of marshmallows and chocolate shavings. Try the delicious recipe for Old-Fashioned Hot Chocolate on page 223. Grown-ups should try it with 2 ounces of white crème de menthe for a new twist on an old favorite.

Taking it to the Limit

Known as The Live Music Capital of the World, Austin has become a musicians' mecca. "Austin City Limits," produced locally by Austin's PBS affiliate, KLRU, has put Austin's music scene on center stage throughout the country for more than a quarter century. In downtown Austin, Sixth Street has the greatest concentration of live music and is home to the nationally known South by Southwest music conference. Austin's relaxed atmosphere lends itself to an easygoing and fun entertaining style. The area, included on the National Register of Historic Districts, bustles with modern restaurants, shops, hotels, and loft apartments in the historic warehouses and buildings from turn-of-the-century Austin.

Put on "Willie Nelson's Greatest Hits" and join us for an evening of food and music to nourish the soul.

Beverage
Ripe Peach Daiquiris

Appetizers
Spicy Spinach Dip
Hill Country Peach Salsa

Soups
Versatile Potato Soup
Butternut Squash and Cauliflower Soup

Salads
Tossed Cobb Salad
Garlic Bread Salad (pictured at right)

Entrées
Fried Venison with Cream Gravy
Chicken Potpie with Cheddar Crust
Fried Catfish

Side Dishes
Green Bean Bundles
Baked Onions au Gratin
Scalloped Potatoes with Garlic and Cream
Cheesy Yellow Squash
Cheese Pie

Bread
Laura Bush's Sweet Potato Biscuits

Desserts
Southern Comfort
Kahlúa Pecan Cakes
Hill Country Peach Ice Cream
Buttermilk Pie
Hill Country Peach Pie
Dripping Springs Pecan Pie

The Texas Hill Country is a beautiful area of rolling hills, rivers, and wide-open skies. It is a place abundant with life. From the explosion of wildflowers in the spring to the vast numbers of animals grazing in the fields, the flora and fauna are overwhelmingly evident in the countryside just outside Austin. Although well known for many of its agricultural products, the Hill Country is most famous for its peaches. In small towns such as Fredericksburg and Stonewall, "peach season" (as summer is known around here) brings visitors from miles around to experience life in these charming communities and to savor the flavor of the delicious fruit. Getting back to life in the city is always a little easier if you take a bushel or two of peaches home with you.

Spicy Spinach Dip

3 (10-ounce) packages frozen chopped spinach, thawed, drained
8 ounces cream cheese, softened
8 ounces grated Parmesan cheese
1 cup mayonnaise
2 tablespoons dried minced onion
1 tablespoon minced fresh garlic
2 teaspoons dried basil
2 teaspoons cayenne pepper
1 pound cheese, shredded, preferably Monterey Jack/Colby blend

Press the excess moisture from the spinach. Combine the cream cheese, Parmesan cheese, mayonnaise, onion, garlic, basil and cayenne pepper in a mixing bowl and beat until blended. Beat in (if your mixer has the capacity) or stir in the spinach and Monterey Jack/Colby cheese. Spoon into a 2-quart baking dish.

Bake at 375 degrees for 45 minutes or until brown and bubbly. Press the top lightly with a paper towel to remove excess oil. Serve warm with tostada chips and/or toasted bread rounds. You may freeze for future use before baking.

Serve as an entrée by spreading the spinach filling on corn tortillas. Roll to enclose the filling. Arrange seam side down in a baking dish and sprinkle with shredded cheese. Bake until heated through.

Serves 15 to 20

Versatile Potato Soup

$^1/_2$ cup (1 stick) butter
8 ribs celery, cut into $^1/_2$-inch slices
1 large white onion, chopped
8 russet potatoes, peeled, cut into quarters
2 quarts hot water
2 cups milk
6 tablespoons flour
3 tablespoons pepper
2 tablespoons salt

Heat the butter in a stockpot until melted. Add the celery and onion and mix well. Cook until the onion is tender, stirring frequently. Add the potatoes and hot water. Bring to a boil. Boil gently for 1 hour, stirring occasionally. Break up the potatoes using a potato masher.

Whisk the milk and flour in a bowl until blended. Add the milk mixture gradually to the potato mixture, stirring constantly. Stir in the pepper and salt. Simmer for 30 minutes, stirring occasionally. Ladle into soup bowls.

Try one or more of these variations as dictated by your taste or guests: Add 1 can chicken broth and the juice of 6 lemons. Serve cold with a sprig of fresh rosemary. Fry bacon and let everyone crumble the desired amount of bacon into his or her soup bowl. Add oysters for a great oyster stew. Add clams for Texas Chowder. Add boiled shrimp, fresh or frozen, and 2 tablespoons Cajun seasoning. Add cheese of choice, sliced venison and/or Elgin hot sausage. The variations are endless. Just be creative.

Serves 8 to 12

Ripe Peach Daiquiris

Combine 3 large pitted unpeeled ripe peaches, one 6-ounce can frozen pink lemonade, 1 lemonade can vodka or rum and 1 to 2 teaspoons confectioners' sugar (depending on the sweetness of the peaches) in a blender. Process until blended. Pour into cocktail glasses. Garnish with sprigs of fresh mint. Serves 4.

Butternut Squash and Cauliflower Soup

1 onion, chopped
1 rib celery, chopped
1 Granny Smith apple, peeled, chopped
1 tablespoon chopped shallots
2 tablespoons vegetable oil
1 teaspoon curry powder, or to taste
$1/2$ teaspoon coriander
8 cups chicken broth
$31/2$ cups chopped peeled butternut squash
Florets of 1 head cauliflower
$11/2$ potatoes, peeled, chopped
$1/4$ cup fresh cilantro leaves, chopped
Salt and pepper to taste
$1/2$ cup sour cream
$1/2$ red bell pepper, julienned
6 deveined peeled shrimp, sautéed or grilled,
 coarsely chopped (optional)

Sauté the onion, celery, apple and shallots in the oil in a stockpot for 5 minutes. Stir in the curry powder and coriander. Cook for several minutes, stirring occasionally. Add the broth and mix well.

Bring to a boil. Stir in the squash, cauliflower and potatoes; reduce heat. Simmer for 20 minutes, stirring occasionally. Process the squash mixture in a blender or food processor until puréed. Stir in the cilantro, salt and pepper. Reheat if desired and serve warm or serve at room temperature. Ladle into soup bowls. Top each serving with sour cream, bell pepper and chopped shrimp.

Serves 8 to 10

Tossed Cobb Salad

12 ounces bleu cheese, crumbled
12 slices crisp-cooked bacon, crumbled
4 hard-cooked eggs, chopped
3 avocados, chopped
2 medium tomatoes, chopped
4 green onions, chopped
French Dressing (in sidebar)
10 cups salad greens

Combine the bleu cheese, bacon, eggs, avocados, tomatoes and green onions in a large salad bowl and mix well. Add the dressing and toss to coat. Add the salad greens and mix well. Serve immediately. You may add 4 cups chopped cooked chicken and serve as an entrée.

Serves 8

Garlic Bread Salad

1/3 cup olive oil
3 garlic cloves, minced
6 (1-inch-thick) slices Italian bread
3 tablespoons balsamic vinegar
4 large Roma tomatoes, cut into 3/4-inch pieces
1 (14-ounce) can artichoke hearts, drained, trimmed
8 ounces fontina cheese, cut into 3/4-inch cubes
4 green onions, thinly sliced
6 to 8 basil leaves, julienned
Salt and pepper to taste

Combine the olive oil and garlic in a bowl and mix well. Reserve half the olive oil mixture. Brush both sides of the bread slices with the remaining olive oil mixture. Arrange the slices in a single layer on a baking sheet. Broil for 2 minutes per side or until light brown. Cut each slice into 1-inch cubes.

Whisk the reserved olive oil mixture and balsamic vinegar in a bowl. Add the bread cubes, tomatoes, artichokes, cheese, green onions and basil and mix gently. Season with salt and pepper. Serve immediately.

Serves 4 to 6

Photograph for this recipe is on page 42.

French Dressing

Combine 1/2 cup olive oil, 1/2 cup salad oil, 1/3 cup balsamic vinegar, 1 tablespoon lemon juice, 1 1/2 teaspoons sugar, 1 teaspoon Worcestershire sauce, 1/2 teaspoon salt, 1/2 teaspoon pepper, 1/2 teaspoon dry mustard and 1 minced garlic clove in a jar with a tight-fitting lid. Cover and shake to mix.

Baked Onions au Gratin

Cook 12 medium onions in boiling salted water in a saucepan for 8 minutes or just until tender; drain. Remove the centers carefully and chop. Arrange the onion shells in a shallow baking dish. Combine the chopped onion centers, 1 cup shredded Cheddar cheese, 2 tablespoons heavy cream, 1/2 teaspoon salt, 1/4 teaspoon pepper and 1/8 teaspoon nutmeg in a bowl and mix well. Spoon the cheese mixture into the onion cavities. Add enough water to the baking dish to measure 1/2 inch. Bake, covered, at 375 degrees for 30 to 35 minutes, removing the cover 5 minutes before the end of the cooking process. Serves 12.

Fried Venison with Cream Gravy

Venison
Venison, trimmed
Milk
Salt and pepper to taste
Flour
Vegetable oil

Cream Gravy
1/4 cup pan drippings
1/4 cup flour
2 to 2 1/2 cups milk
1/2 teaspoon salt
1/8 teaspoon pepper

For the venison, cut the venison against the grain into 1/2-inch slices. Arrange the slices in a dish. Pour enough milk over the venison to cover. Soak, covered, in the refrigerator for 8 to 10 hours; drain. Pound the slices between sheets of waxed paper with a meat mallet to tenderize. Combine salt, pepper and flour in a sealable plastic bag. Add the venison and shake to coat.

Fry the venison in hot oil in a skillet until golden brown on both sides and cooked through. Drain, reserving 1/4 cup of the pan drippings for the gravy. Arrange the venison on a platter and cover to keep warm.

For the gravy, combine the reserved pan drippings and flour in a skillet and mix well. Cook over low heat until bubbly, stirring constantly. Add the milk gradually, stirring constantly. Cook until thickened, stirring constantly. Season with the salt and pepper. Serve with the venison.

Variable servings

Chicken Potpie with Cheddar Crust

Cheese Pastry

4 cups flour
2 cups shredded sharp Cheddar cheese
1 1/2 cups (3 sticks) butter, chilled, chopped
2/3 cup ice water
2 egg yolks, beaten
1/4 cup cream

Filling and Assembly

6 tablespoons butter
6 tablespoons flour
2 cups chicken broth
1 cup cream
1/2 teaspoon freshly ground pepper
Salt to taste
8 ounces sausage (optional)
4 cups chopped cooked chicken
1 cup sliced mushrooms, sautéed
1 to 2 cups vegetables of choice, blanched

For the pastry, process the flour, cheese and butter in a food processor until crumbly. Add the ice water gradually, processing constantly until the mixture forms a ball. Chill, wrapped in plastic wrap, for 1 hour. Divide the dough into 2 equal portions. Roll each portion into a 12-inch circle on a lightly floured circle. Brush each portion with a mixture of the egg yolks and cream.

For the filling, heat the butter in a skillet until melted. Stir in the flour. Cook for 2 minutes, stirring constantly. Add the broth and cream gradually, stirring constantly. Stir in the pepper and salt. Cook for 5 minutes or until thick and smooth and of a sauce consistency, stirring constantly. Remove from heat. Brown the sausage in a skillet, stirring until crumbly; drain. Stir the sausage, chicken, mushrooms and blanched vegetables into the white sauce.

To assemble, fit 1 of the pastry circles into a 9-inch pie plate. Spoon the filling into the prepared pie plate. Top with the remaining pastry, fluting the edge and cutting vents. Bake at 425 degrees for 25 to 30 minutes or until brown.

Serves 6

Combine 4 chopped
peeled Fredericksburg peaches,
2 chopped seeded jalapeño
chiles, 2 tablespoons fresh lime
juice and 2 tablespoons chopped
fresh cilantro in a bowl and mix
gently. Let stand, covered, for
several hours to allow the flavors
to meld. Serve with pork, chicken
or grilled fish.

Fried Catfish

8 whole catfish, cleaned, dressed
Lemon juice
2^1/$_2$ cups flour
2 teaspoons salt
1 tablespoon paprika
1 (12-ounce) can beer
Vegetable oil
Sprigs of parsley (optional)
Lemon wedges (optional)

Rinse the catfish with cold water and pat dry. Arrange in a large shallow dish. Drizzle both sides of the catfish with lemon juice. Chill, covered, for 20 minutes.

Mix half the flour and half the salt in a shallow dish. Coat the catfish with the flour mixture. Combine the remaining flour, remaining salt and paprika in a bowl and mix well. Stir in the beer. Dip the catfish in the batter. Heat oil in a deep fryer to 375 degrees. Deep-fry the catfish in the hot oil until the catfish float to the top and are golden brown; drain. Arrange on a serving platter. Top with sprigs of parsley and lemon wedges.

Serves 8

Green Bean Bundles

1 pound fresh green beans, trimmed
4 slices bacon
^{1}/$_2$ cup packed brown sugar
^{1}/$_4$ cup (^{1}/$_2$ stick) butter, melted
^{1}/$_2$ garlic clove, crushed

Blanch the beans in boiling water in a saucepan for 3 minutes; drain. Plunge the beans into a bowl of ice water to stop the cooking process; drain.

Divide the beans into 4 equal portions. Wrap each portion with 1 slice of bacon and secure with a wooden pick. Arrange the bundles in a 1^1/$_2$-quart baking dish. Combine the brown sugar, melted butter and garlic in a bowl and mix well. Drizzle over the beans. Bake at 350 degrees for 30 minutes.

Serves 4

Scalloped Potatoes with Garlic and Cream

2 pounds red waxy boiling potatoes, peeled, thinly sliced
1$^1/_2$ cups milk
1$^1/_2$ cups heavy cream
2 to 4 garlic cloves, mashed
$^1/_2$ to $^3/_4$ teaspoon salt
$^1/_2$ teaspoon white pepper
$^1/_2$ to 1 teaspoon freshly grated nutmeg
2 tablespoons unsalted butter
1 cup (or more) shredded imported Swiss, Emmentaler or Gruyère cheese

Combine the potatoes, milk, heavy cream, garlic, salt, white pepper and nutmeg in a saucepan. Bring to a simmer, stirring occasionally. Pour into a buttered shallow gratin dish. Dot with the butter and sprinkle with the cheese. Bake at 375 degrees for 1 hour or until the potatoes are tender and brown.

Serves 4 to 6

Cheesy Yellow Squash

1$^1/_2$ pounds yellow squash, sliced
1 large onion, chopped
1 teaspoon sugar
$^1/_2$ teaspoon salt
Butter to taste, softened
4 eggs, lightly beaten
$^3/_4$ cup (or more) shredded Cheddar cheese
$^1/_2$ cup milk
$^1/_4$ cup bread crumbs
$^1/_8$ teaspoon cayenne pepper
Freshly grated Parmesan cheese to taste

Combine the squash, onion, sugar and salt with enough water to cover in a saucepan. Bring to a boil; reduce heat. Cook until the squash and onion are tender; drain. Spoon the squash mixture into a bowl and mash. Add butter and mix well. Stir in the eggs. Add the Cheddar cheese, milk, bread crumbs and cayenne pepper and mix well. Spoon into a buttered 8×8-inch baking dish. Sprinkle with Parmesan cheese. Bake at 350 degrees for 30 minutes or until brown and bubbly.

Serves 4

Cheese Pie

2 refrigerated pie pastries
1$1/4$ cups ricotta cheese
8 ounces mozzarella cheese, cubed
5$1/3$ ounces smoked provolone cheese, cubed
1$2/3$ cups grated Parmesan cheese
4 ounces prosciutto, chopped
$1/4$ cup chopped fresh flat-leaf parsley
4 eggs, beaten
1 teaspoon pepper

Fit 1 of the pie pastries into a 9-inch pie plate. Combine the ricotta cheese, mozzarella cheese, provolone cheese, Parmesan cheese, prosciutto, parsley, eggs and pepper in a bowl and mix well. Spoon into the pastry-lined pie plate. Top with the remaining pastry, fluting the edge and cutting vents. Bake at 325 to 350 degrees for 1 hour. Let stand for 30 minutes before serving.

Serves 6 to 8

Laura Bush's Sweet Potato Biscuits

1 cup flour
2 teaspoons baking powder
2 teaspoons sugar
$1/4$ teaspoon salt
3 tablespoons butter, chilled
1 cup cold mashed cooked sweet potato
Milk, melted butter or cream

Combine the flour, baking powder, sugar and salt in a bowl and mix well. Cut in the butter until crumbly. Add the sweet potato and mix well. Pat the dough $3/4$ inch thick on a lightly floured surface. Cut with a 2$1/2$-inch biscuit cutter. Arrange the biscuits on a greased baking sheet. Brush the tops with milk. Bake at 375 degrees for 15 minutes or just until the biscuits begin to brown.

Makes 1 dozen biscuits

Southern Comfort

1 1/2 cups flour
1/2 cup packed brown sugar
1 cup (2 sticks) butter, melted
1 1/2 cups chopped pecans
1 jar caramel ice cream topping
1/2 gallon ice cream or frozen yogurt, softened
1/2 cup scotch (optional)
1 jar caramel ice cream topping (optional)

Combine the flour and brown sugar in a bowl and mix well. Stir in the butter. Add the pecans and mix well. Spread the pecan mixture in a thin layer on a baking sheet. Bake at 350 degrees for 20 to 30 minutes or until crisp. Cool slightly and crumble.

Spread half the crumbled pecan mixture in a 9×12-inch dish. Layer with half of 1 jar of the caramel ice cream topping, ice cream, remaining 1/2 jar caramel ice cream topping and remaining pecan mixture in the order listed. Freeze, covered, until firm. Cut into squares.

Heat the scotch and 1 jar caramel ice cream topping in a saucepan until warm, stirring frequently. Drizzle over each serving.

Serves 15

Kahlúa Pecan Cakes

1/2 cup (1 stick) unsalted butter
1/2 cup semisweet chocolate chips
3/4 cup sugar
1/2 cup flour
2 eggs, beaten
1 tablespoon Kahlúa
1 teaspoon instant espresso powder
1/2 cup chopped pecans
24 large pecan halves

Combine the butter and chocolate chips in a double boiler. Cook until blended, stirring frequently. Remove from heat. Let stand until cool. Whisk in the sugar, flour, eggs, Kahlúa and espresso powder until smooth. Stir in the pecans. Line 24 miniature muffin cups with paper liners. Fill the prepared muffin cups 2/3 full. Top each with 1 pecan half. Bake at 350 degrees for 20 minutes. Remove to a wire rack to cool.

Makes 2 dozen

*How to Make a
Hill Country Peach Pie*

Fit 1 refrigerated pie pastry into a 9-inch pie plate. Unwrap 1 frozen pie filling (page 55) and place in the prepared pie plate. Roll another refrigerated pie pastry on a lightly floured surface to press out the fold lines. Place over the top of the peach mixture. Fold the edge under and crimp. Cut slits in the top pastry. Bake at 425 degrees for 15 minutes. Cover the edge of the pastry with foil. Bake for 25 to 30 minutes longer or until golden brown. Cool on a wire rack. If the filling is not frozen, bake as directed, reducing the second baking time to 20 minutes.

Hill Country Peach Ice Cream

$2^1/4$ cups sugar
$1/3$ cup flour
$1/8$ teaspoon salt
4 cups half-and-half
2 (12-ounce) cans evaporated milk
6 eggs, lightly beaten
4 to 6 cups sliced peeled fresh peaches
$3/4$ cup sugar
3 tablespoons vanilla extract
2 teaspoons almond extract

Combine $2^1/4$ cups sugar, flour and salt in a large saucepan and mix well. Stir in the half-and-half, evaporated milk and eggs. Cook over medium heat until the mixture is hot and begins to thicken, stirring constantly. Remove from heat. Let stand until cool. You may prepare up to this point and store, covered, in the refrigerator for 8 to 10 hours.

Combine the peaches and $3/4$ cup sugar in a blender or food processor. Process just until the peaches are finely chopped. Let stand for 30 minutes. Stir the peach mixture and flavorings into the milk mixture. Pour the milk mixture into a 5-quart ice cream freezer container. Freeze using manufacturer's directions.

Serves 15 to 20

Buttermilk Pie

1¹/₄ cups sugar
¹/₂ cup (1 stick) butter, softened
3 eggs, beaten
3 tablespoons (rounded) flour
1 cup buttermilk
1 teaspoon vanilla extract
1 unbaked (9-inch) pie shell
¹/₄ teaspoon nutmeg (optional)

Beat the sugar and butter with a mixer fitted with a wire whisk until creamy, scraping the bowl occasionally. Add the eggs and flour and beat until blended. Stir in the buttermilk and vanilla. Spoon into the pie shell. Sprinkle with the nutmeg. Bake at 350 degrees for 40 to 50 minutes or until a knife inserted in the center comes out clean.

Serves 8

Dripping Springs Pecan Pie

1 cup (6 ounces) semisweet chocolate chips (optional)
1 unbaked (9-inch) pie shell
1 cup corn syrup
1 cup sugar
1 teaspoon salt
3 eggs, lightly beaten
2 tablespoons butter, melted
1 tablespoon vanilla extract
1 cup pecan halves

Sprinkle the chocolate chips over the bottom of the pie shell. Combine the corn syrup, sugar and salt in a bowl and mix well. Stir in the eggs, butter and vanilla. Add the pecans and mix gently. Spoon into the prepared pie shell. Bake at 400 degrees for 15 minutes. Reduce the oven temperature to 350 degrees. Bake for 45 minutes longer or until set.

Serves 6 to 8

Hill Country Peach Pie Filling

Stock your freezer with Hill Country Peach Pie Filling when Fredericksburg peaches are in season. Then when you are ready for some peach pie, simply place the filling in a prepared pie shell (page 53) and bake. To prepare, toss 5 cups sliced peeled Hill Country peaches with 1¹/₂ teaspoons lemon juice in a bowl. Sprinkle with a mixture of 1 cup sugar, ¹/₄ cup flour and ¹/₂ teaspoon cinnamon and toss gently. Line a 9-inch pie plate with heavy-duty plastic wrap, allowing a 6- to 8-inch overhang. Spoon the filling into the prepared pie plate. Drizzle with 2 tablespoons melted butter. Fold the edge of the plastic wrap over the top and seal securely. Freeze until firm. Remove the filling from the pie plate and wrap in foil. Freeze for up to 1 year.

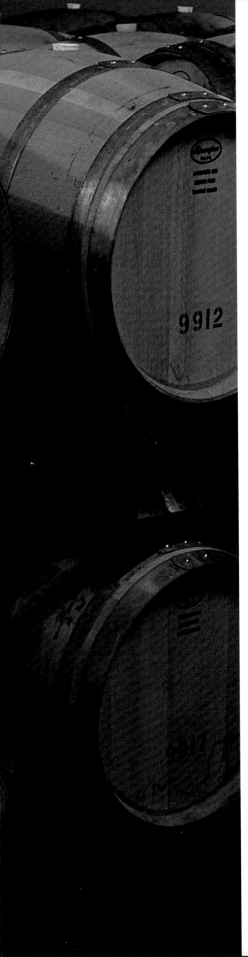

You've got to have *Friends*

The European wine-making tradition, first brought to the Texas Hill Country in the nineteenth century, has enjoyed a renaissance as a growing number of wineries, such as Fall Creek Vineyards just outside of Austin, have established roots in central Texas. The Texas Food and Wine Festival held each spring brings a sampling of some of the area's—and country's—best chefs and vintners to Austin for a weekend of great food, good spirits, and lots of fun. In addition to a growing national reputation for its wine, central Texas is home to several microbreweries and brewpubs.

Menu

La Vida Dolce—an evening of good friends, good food, and good wine!

Beverages
    Rosé Sangria
    Champagne Cocktail

Appetizers
    Eggplant and Goat Cheese Sandwiches with
       Tomato Tarragon Sauce
    Mushrooms Parmesan
    Goat Cheese, Pine Nut and Sun-Dried Phyllo Cups

Soup
    Garlic Soup

Salad
    Caesar Salad with Olive Sticks

Entrées
    Chicken Marbella
    Paella Valenciana
    Eggplant Parmesan

Side Dishes
    Smoked Gouda Risotto with Spinach and Mushrooms
    Broccoli with Sun-Dried Tomatoes and Pine Nuts
    Portobello Bread Pudding
    Basic Pesto
    Stuffed Red Peppers

Breads
    Caramelized Onion, Goat Cheese and Dried Fig Pizza
    Basil Pesto and Roasted Pepper Pizza (pictured at right)
    Pizza with a Neapolitan Twist (pictured at right)
    Focaccia

Desserts
    Chocolate Gelato
    Creamy Lemon Gelato
    Vanilla Gelato
    Chocolate Italian Cream Cake

Antipasto means before the pasta. The word "antipasti" is used to describe assorted cold Italian hors d'oeuvre arranged on a platter and served before a meal. Most antipasti arrangements will include smoked meats (such as Parma ham or prosciutto); various cheeses; and a variety of olives, peppers, and other marinated vegetables (such as artichoke hearts or mushrooms). Another interesting element to include is fruit; dates, fresh figs, or strawberries give a sweet alternative to the salty flavors of the meat and the vinegar taste of the vegetable marinade. An antipasti is always a great appetizer option because it requires little maintenance once it's arranged and the large variety of food assures there's something for everyone.

Eggplant and Goat Cheese Sandwiches with Tomato Tarragon Sauce

Tomato Tarragon Sauce

1 tablespoon olive oil
1 small onion, chopped
1 (28-ounce) can crushed tomatoes in purée
$1^1/2$ teaspoons dried tarragon
1 teaspoon sugar
$3/4$ teaspoon salt
$1/4$ teaspoon freshly ground pepper

Eggplant and Goat Cheese Sandwiches

1 cup dry bread crumbs
$1/2$ cup grated Parmesan cheese
$1/2$ teaspoon salt
$1/4$ teaspoon freshly ground pepper
2 eggplant, peeled, cut into sixteen $1/2$-inch slices
4 eggs, beaten
Vegetable oil
8 ounces mild goat cheese, such as Montrachet, cut into 8 rounds

For the sauce, heat the olive oil in a saucepan until hot. Add the onion. Cook for 5 minutes or until tender, stirring occasionally. Stir in the tomatoes, tarragon, sugar and salt. Simmer for 25 minutes, stirring occasionally. Stir in the pepper. Remove from heat. Cover to keep warm.

For the sandwiches, combine the bread crumbs, Parmesan cheese, salt and pepper in a bowl and mix well. Dip the eggplant in the eggs and coat with the bread crumb mixture. Pour enough oil into a skillet to measure $1/2$ inch. Heat over medium heat until hot. Fry the eggplant in batches in the hot oil for 1 to 2 minutes per side or until golden brown and cooked through; drain.

Arrange half the eggplant in a single layer on a baking sheet. Place 1 round of goat cheese on each slice. Top with the remaining eggplant slices. Bake at 350 degrees for 10 minutes or until the cheese melts.

To assemble, puddle some of the sauce on each of 8 serving plates. Top each serving with 1 sandwich.

Makes 8 sandwiches

Mushrooms Parmesan

24 fresh medium mushroom caps
2 tablespoons butter
8 ounces spicy pork sausage
1 onion, chopped
1 garlic clove, minced
1/2 cup finely crushed butter crackers
1/3 cup chicken stock

3 tablespoons grated Parmesan
   cheese
1 tablespoon chopped fresh parsley
1/2 teaspoon salt
1/4 teaspoon dried oregano
Pepper to taste

Sauté the mushrooms in the butter in a skillet briefly. Using a slotted spoon, remove the mushrooms to a bowl, reserving the pan drippings. Add the sausage, onion and garlic to the pan drippings. Cook until the sausage is cooked through and the onion is tender, stirring frequently; do not brown. Stir in the cracker crumbs, stock, cheese, parsley, salt, oregano and pepper.

Spoon the sausage mixture into the mushroom caps, rounding the tops. Arrange the mushrooms in a single layer in a shallow baking pan. Add enough water to the baking pan to measure 1/4 inch. Bake at 325 degrees for 15 minutes or until heated through.

Makes 2 dozen

Goat Cheese, Pine Nut and Sun-Dried Tomato Phyllo Cups

8 ounces mild goat cheese
4 ounces cream cheese, softened
3 eggs
1/3 cup pine nuts, toasted
1/4 cup packed finely chopped
   sun-dried tomatoes

6 scallions with tops, finely chopped
2 tablespoons finely chopped fresh
   dill
Salt to taste
Freshly ground pepper to taste
36 phyllo cups

Combine the goat cheese and cream cheese in a bowl and mix until blended. Add the eggs 1 at a time, mixing well after each addition. Stir in the pine nuts, sun-dried tomatoes, scallions, dill, salt and pepper. You may prepare in advance up to this point and store, covered, in the refrigerator. Bring to room temperature before proceeding with the recipe.

Place each phyllo cup in a miniature muffin cup. Fill each phyllo cup 3/4 full. Bake at 350 degrees for 12 to 15 minutes or until the pastry is golden brown and the filling puffs. Remove to a wire rack to cool.

Makes 3 dozen

Champagne Cocktail

Place 1 sugar cube in a glass. Add a dash of angostura bitters and gradually fill the glass with Champagne. Serve with a maraschino cherry and a lemon twist (a $1/4 \times 1$-inch strip of the yellow peel). A simple way to serve these is to put out the ingredients and let the guests make their own. Serves 1.

Garlic Soup

2 large brown onions, coarsely chopped
3 ribs celery, coarsely chopped
1 large carrot, peeled, coarsely chopped
1 large parsnip, peeled, coarsely chopped
$1/4$ cup vegetable oil
10 cups chicken or vegetable stock, heated
$1^1/4$ pounds russet potatoes, peeled, coarsely chopped
1 pound (4 large heads) garlic, cut horizontally into halves
Bouquet garni (5 sprigs of Italian parsley, 3 sprigs of thyme
    and 1 sprig of rosemary tied in cheesecloth)
Kosher salt to taste
Freshly cracked pepper to taste
8 ounces broccoli rabe
1 tablespoon vegetable oil
$1/4$ teaspoon kosher salt
Extra-virgin olive oil

Sauté the onions, celery, carrot and parsnip in $1/4$ cup vegetable oil in a stockpot over medium-high heat for 10 minutes or until light brown. Stir in the stock. Add the potatoes, garlic and bouquet garni. Simmer for 1 hour or until the vegetables and garlic are tender, stirring occasionally. Discard the bouquet garni.

Process the soup in batches in a blender or food mill until puréed. Strain into a clean stockpot through a coarse mesh stainless steel strainer. Season with kosher salt to taste and pepper. Cover and keep warm over low heat. You may prepare up to this point and chill, covered, for up to 3 days before continuing with the recipe.

Cut off the top 2 inches of each broccoli rabe stalk, reserving the tops and discarding the remaining portion. Heat 1 tablespoon vegetable oil in a sauté pan over high heat to the smoking point. Sauté the broccoli rabe tops for 4 minutes or until light brown. Sprinkle with $1/4$ teaspoon kosher salt.

Ladle about 8 ounces of the soup into each of 8 to 10 heated soup bowls. Add some of the broccoli rabe to each serving and drizzle with extra-virgin olive oil. Serve immediately.

Serves 8 to 10

Caesar Salad

2 or 3 garlic cloves, minced
Salt and freshly ground pepper to
   taste
4 anchovy fillets, mashed (optional)
6 tablespoons olive oil
$1^1/2$ tablespoons lemon juice
1 teaspoon Worcestershire sauce

1 teaspoon Dijon mustard
1 egg yolk, lightly beaten or
   equivalent amount of egg substitute
$^1/8$ to $^1/4$ teaspoon hot sauce
1 or 2 heads romaine, torn
Freshly grated Parmesan cheese
Croutons (optional)

Rub the side and bottom of a wooden salad bowl with the garlic. Sprinkle with salt and pepper. Combine the anchovies, olive oil, lemon juice, Worcestershire sauce, Dijon mustard, egg yolk and hot sauce in the prepared salad bowl and mix well. Add the romaine and toss to coat. Sprinkle with cheese and pepper. Top with croutons. Serve immediately with Olive Sticks (below).

Serves 4 to 6

Olive Sticks

8 ounces feta cheese, drained,
   crumbled
$^1/3$ cup minced fresh parsley
$^1/3$ cup olive paste

2 egg whites
1 (17-ounce) package frozen puff
   pastry, thawed

Combine the feta cheese, parsley, olive paste and egg whites in a bowl and mix well. Unfold 1 of the pastry sheets on a lightly floured surface, keeping the remaining pastry sheet in the refrigerator. Roll into a 14×16-inch rectangle with a floured rolling pin. Cut crosswise into halves. Spread half the olive mixture over 1 pastry half. Top with the remaining pastry half. Roll gently with a rolling pin to seal the layers together. Cut the pastry crosswise into $^1/2$-inch-wide strips. Arrange the strips 1 inch apart on a greased baking sheet, twisting each strip 3 or 4 times. Bake at 400 degrees for 12 to 15 minutes or until puffed and light brown. Remove to a wire rack to cool completely. Repeat the process with the remaining puff pastry and remaining olive mixture.

Serve at room temperature. Store in a tightly covered container. You may substitute a mixture of $^1/2$ cup puréed pitted kalamata olives and 1 tablespoon olive oil for the olive paste.

Makes 56 olive sticks

Chicken Marbella

3 large chickens, cut into quarters
1 cup packed brown sugar
1/2 cup olive oil
1/2 cup balsamic vinegar
1 cup prunes, pitted
1/2 cup chopped fresh basil
1/2 cup pitted green olives
1/2 cup capers
2 tablespoons minced garlic
Salt and pepper to taste
1 cup dry white wine
1/2 cup chopped flat-leaf parsley

Place the chicken quarters in sealable plastic bags. Combine the brown sugar, olive oil and balsamic vinegar in a bowl and mix well. Stir in the prunes, basil, green olives, capers, garlic, salt and pepper. Pour over the chickens and seal tightly. Marinate in the refrigerator for 8 to 10 hours, turning the bags occasionally.

Arrange the undrained chicken quarters in a single layer in a large baking pan. Drizzle with the wine. Bake at 350 degrees for 1 hour, basting frequently. Remove the chicken and sauce to a serving platter. Sprinkle with the parsley. You may substitute 2 or 3 heads of roasted garlic squeezed out of the cloves for the 2 tablespoons minced garlic.

Serves 12

Paella Valenciana

1 pound chorizo sausage
3 cups chicken broth
$^1/_2$ cup white wine
1 tablespoon thyme
1 bay leaf
3 pounds boneless skinless chicken
   breasts or thighs
Salt and pepper to taste
8 ounces boneless pork chops
$^2/_3$ cup extra-virgin olive oil
2 large yellow onions, chopped
2 green bell peppers, julienned
2 red bell peppers, julienned
2 (10-ounce) cans artichokes,
   drained, rinsed, cut into halves
8 scallions, chopped

6 garlic cloves, mashed
$^1/_2$ teaspoon paprika
$1^1/_2$ pounds medium shrimp
1 pound sea or bay scallops
1 pound fresh squid, sliced into rings
5 cups long grain rice
2 large tomatoes, seeded, chopped
$1^1/_2$ teaspoons saffron threads
10 cups chicken broth, heated
$^1/_2$ cup chopped Italian parsley
2 bay leaves
$^1/_2$ cup dry white wine
2 teaspoons salt, or to taste
$^1/_2$ teaspoon pepper, or to taste
3 dozen fresh clams, steamed
3 dozen fresh mussels, steamed

Combine the sausage, 3 cups broth, $^1/_2$ cup wine, thyme and 1 bay leaf in a large saucepan. Simmer for 20 minutes. Drain, reserving the sausage. Slice the sausage. Divide all of the ingredients between two 12- to 15-inch shallow-sided paella pans, skillets or sauté pans to speed up the cooking process. Cut each piece of chicken into 3 or 4 pieces. Sprinkle with salt and pepper to taste. Cut the pork chops into 1-inch pieces.

Sauté the chicken in the olive oil in the paella pans for 5 to 10 minutes or just until the chicken is almost tender. Remove the chicken with a slotted spoon to a large bowl, reserving the pan drippings. Add the sausage and pork to the reserved pan drippings. Sauté for 4 minutes per side. Remove the sausage and pork with a slotted spoon to the bowl containing the chicken, reserving the pan drippings. Add the onions, bell peppers, artichokes, scallions and garlic and mix well. Sauté for 8 minutes. Stir in the paprika. Remove the vegetable mixture with a slotted spoon to the chicken mixture, reserving the pan drippings. You may prepare up to this point several hours in advance and store, covered, in the refrigerator.

Peel and devein the shrimp, leaving the tails intact. Add the shrimp, scallops and squid to the reserved pan drippings. Sauté for 1 minute. Remove with a slotted spoon to the chicken mixture, reserving the pan drippings. Add additional olive oil if necessary and heat until hot. Add the rice and stir until coated. Stir in the tomatoes. Cook just until heated through. Add the saffron, 10 cups warm broth, parsley, 2 bay leaves, $^1/_2$ cup wine, 2 teaspoons salt and $^1/_2$ teaspoon pepper and mix well. Bring to a boil; reduce heat to medium. Cook for 10 minutes, stirring occasionally; the rice will not be tender. Spoon the rice mixture into the bowl with the chicken mixture and mix well, adding additional broth if needed to moisten. Spoon the mixture into 2 paella pans. Bake at 350 degrees for 10 to 15 minutes or until the rice is tender; remove the bay leaves. Stir the top layer of rice to moisten. Arrange the clams and mussels in their shells on top just before serving.

Serves 18 to 25

Rosé Sangria

Arrange 6 ounces assorted grapes (Muscat, black, red, or green) in a single layer on a baking sheet; do not allow grapes to touch. Freeze for 8 to 10 hours or until frozen solid. Combine 24 ounces rosé, 3¹/₂ ounces grapefruit juice, 3¹/₂ ounces tequila, 3¹/₂ ounces cranberry juice and ¹/₄ cup plus 3 tablespoons superfine sugar in a 3-quart pitcher and mix well. Add the frozen grapes. Pour over ice in glasses. Makes 6 (6-ounce) servings.

Eggplant Parmesan

Tomato Sauce
2 garlic cloves, minced
2 tablespoons chopped fresh parsley
2 tablespoons olive oil
1 (14-ounce) can diced tomatoes
¹/₂ cup water
¹/₃ cup tomato paste
¹/₂ teaspoon dried oregano
¹/₂ teaspoon pepper

Eggplant and Assembly
¹/₂ cup (or more) flour
¹/₂ teaspoon salt
1 medium eggplant, peeled, cut into ¹/₂-inch slices
1 egg, beaten
3 tablespoons vegetable oil
¹/₃ cup grated Parmesan cheese
4 ounces mozzarella cheese, shredded
4 ounces mozzarella cheese, cut into triangles

For the sauce, sauté the garlic and parsley in the olive oil in a saucepan over medium heat until the garlic is tender. Stir in the undrained tomatoes, water, tomato paste, oregano and pepper. Simmer for 20 minutes or until thickened, stirring occasionally and adding additional water if needed for a thinner consistency.

For the eggplant, mix the flour and salt in a shallow dish. Dip the eggplant slices in the egg and coat with the flour mixture, shaking to remove any excess flour. Heat the oil in a skillet over medium heat until hot. Add the eggplant. Cook for 2 to 3 minutes on each side or until light brown, adding additional oil if needed; drain.

To assemble, line the bottom of a 10×12-inch or 9×9-inch baking pan with half the eggplant, cutting the slices if needed to fit. Sprinkle with half the Parmesan cheese. Spread with half the sauce and sprinkle with 4 ounces shredded mozzarella cheese. Top with the remaining eggplant slices, remaining Parmesan cheese and remaining sauce. Arrange the mozzarella cheese triangles over the top. Bake at 400 degrees for 20 to 25 minutes or until bubbly.

Serves 4

Smoked Gouda Risotto with Spinach and Mushrooms

Risotto

2 (16-ounce) cans nonfat reduced-sodium chicken broth
2 cups water
1 tablespoon butter
$1/3$ cup chopped shallots
2 cups arborio rice or any short grain rice
$1/2$ cup dry white wine
$1/2$ teaspoon salt
$1^1/2$ cups shredded smoked Gouda cheese
5 cups (5 ounces) chopped fresh spinach

Mushrooms and Assembly

1 tablespoon olive oil
2 cups ($3^1/2$ ounces) sliced shiitake mushrooms
3 cups (8 ounces) sliced button mushrooms
2 cups (8 ounces) sliced cremini mushrooms
2 cups ($3^1/2$ ounces) sliced oyster mushrooms
$1/3$ cup chopped shallots
$1/4$ cup dry white wine
$1^1/2$ teaspoons chopped fresh thyme
$1^1/2$ teaspoons chopped fresh rosemary
1 garlic clove, minced
$1/4$ teaspoon each salt and pepper
$1/4$ cup freshly grated Parmesan cheese
Sprigs of fresh rosemary

For the risotto, combine the broth and water in a bowl. Heat the butter in a nonstick saucepan over medium heat until melted. Stir in the shallots. Cook, covered, for 2 minutes. Stir in the rice. Cook for 2 minutes, stirring constantly. Stir in the wine. Cook for 30 seconds or until the wine is almost absorbed, stirring constantly. Stir in the salt. Add $1/2$ cup of the broth mixture and mix well. Cook until the liquid is absorbed, stirring constantly. Add the remaining broth mixture $1/2$ cup at a time, cooking until the broth is absorbed after each addition and stirring constantly. The process should take about 20 minutes. Stir in the cheese. Cook just until melted, stirring constantly. Stir in the spinach. Cook just until the spinach wilts, stirring constantly.

For the mushrooms, heat the olive oil in a large nonstick skillet over medium-high heat. Add the mushrooms. Sauté for 5 minutes or just until the mushrooms begin to brown. Add the shallots, wine, thyme, rosemary and garlic and mix well. Sauté for 1 minute or until the wine is absorbed. Sprinkle with the salt and pepper.

To assemble, spoon 1 cup of the risotto into each of 6 bowls. Top each serving with 1 cup of the mushroom mixture. Sprinkle with the Parmesan cheese. Garnish with sprigs of fresh rosemary.

Serves 6

Broccoli with Sun-Dried Tomatoes and Pine Nuts

Florets of 1 bunch broccoli
8 oil-pack sun-dried tomatoes, drained, slivered
2 garlic cloves, minced
1 tablespoon olive oil
2/3 cup pine nuts, toasted
Salt and pepper to taste

Combine the broccoli with enough water to cover in a saucepan. Boil until tender-crisp; drain. Plunge the broccoli into ice water to stop the cooking process; drain. You may prepare up to this point early in the day and chill, covered, until just before serving.

Sauté the sun-dried tomatoes and garlic in the olive oil in a skillet until the garlic is light brown. Add the broccoli. Sauté just until heated through. Stir in the pine nuts. Season with salt and pepper. Serve immediately.

Serves 4

Portobello Bread Pudding

3 cups dry (1/2-inch) French bread cubes
1 tablespoon chopped garlic
1/4 cup (or less) olive oil
2 cups chopped spinach
1 pound portobello mushrooms, stemmed, thinly sliced
1 cup grated Parmigiano-Reggiano
4 eggs
3/4 cup half-and-half
3/4 cup heavy cream
1 teaspoon kosher salt
1/4 teaspoon pepper

Spread the bread cubes in a 2 1/2-quart round baking dish. Sauté the garlic in 1 tablespoon of the olive oil in a skillet until the garlic is light brown. Combine with the spinach in a bowl and mix well. Spoon over the bread cubes.

Sear the mushrooms on both sides in 2 to 3 tablespoons of the olive oil in a skillet and arrange slightly overlapping in a circle over the spinach. Sprinkle with the cheese. Whisk the eggs, half-and-half, heavy cream, kosher salt and pepper in a bowl until blended. Pour over the top. Bake at 350 degrees for 30 minutes.

Serves 4 to 6

Basic Pesto

2 cups packed fresh basil leaves
1 cup olive oil
1 cup grated Parmesan cheese
1/2 cup pine nuts, toasted
6 to 8 garlic cloves

Combine the basil, olive oil, Parmesan cheese, pine nuts and garlic in a food processor. Process until smooth or until of the desired consistency. Store, covered, in the refrigerator.

Makes 1 to 2 cups

Stuffed Red Peppers

3 red bell peppers
1 1/2 tablespoons balsamic vinegar
1 1/2 teaspoons olive oil
1 garlic clove, minced
Salt and pepper to taste
12 ounces cherry tomatoes, cut into halves
1 cup shredded mozzarella cheese
1/2 cup loosely packed fresh basil, julienned

Slice the bell peppers lengthwise into halves. Remove the seeds and membranes. Whisk the balsamic vinegar, olive oil, garlic, salt and pepper in a bowl. Stir in the cherry tomatoes, cheese and basil.

Spoon the tomato mixture into the bell pepper halves. Arrange the bell peppers cut side up on a baking sheet sprayed with nonstick cooking spray. Bake at 375 degrees for 40 minutes or until the bell peppers are tender. Serve with pasta or grilled chicken.

Serves 6

Pesto is a wonderful innovation. Its versatility makes it a necessity for every kitchen. Although there are many different flavors available for purchase, pesto is very easy to make at home. The herb most frequently used is fresh basil, but experiment with others to suit your own tastes.

Basil Pesto and Roasted Pepper Pizza

Spread 1 (9-inch) prepared pizza crust (see recipe at right) with 4 ounces basil pesto. Sprinkle with $1/2$ julienned roasted red bell pepper, $1/3$ cup kalamata olive halves and 6 ounces crumbled feta cheese. Bake using crust directions.

Pizza with a Neapolitan Twist

Arrange 6 large julienned basil leaves on 1 prepared (9-inch) pizza crust (see recipe at right). Layer with 2 thinly sliced large ripe tomatoes, $1/3$ cup roasted garlic cloves and 8 ounces thinly sliced Brie cheese. Bake using crust directions.

Photograph for these recipes is on page 58.

Caramelized Onion, Goat Cheese and Dried Fig Pizza

Crust
1 envelope dry yeast
$1/2$ teaspoon sugar
$3/4$ cup warm (110 degrees) water
2 to $2^1/4$ cups flour
1 teaspoon salt
2 tablespoons olive oil

Topping
2 large onions, sliced, separated into rings
3 tablespoons olive oil
2 tablespoons minced garlic
2 tablespoons sugar
2 tablespoons balsamic vinegar
1 tablespoon salt
6 ounces goat cheese, crumbled
8 to 10 dried figs, cut into quarters

For the crust, dissolve the yeast and sugar in the warm water in a bowl, letting stand for 5 minutes or until foamy. Mound the flour on a hard work surface and make a well in the center of the flour. Add the salt and 1 tablespoon of the olive oil to the well. Add the yeast mixture to the well gradually, stirring constantly with a fork until the mixture adheres and is of a dough consistency. Shape the dough into a ball and reflour the work surface. Knead for 10 minutes or until smooth and elastic.

Coat the side and bottom of a bowl with the remaining 1 tablespoon olive oil. Place the dough in the bowl, turning to coat the surface. Let rise, covered with plastic wrap, for 2 hours or until doubled in bulk.

Roll the dough on a lightly floured surface to the desired thickness, making a lip around the outer edge. Arrange on a baking sheet or pizza stone. Let rise, covered, for 20 to 30 minutes.

For the topping, sauté the onions in the olive oil in a skillet over medium heat until tender. Add the garlic and sugar and mix well. Sauté for 5 to 10 minutes longer or until golden brown and caramelized, stirring frequently. Stir in the balsamic vinegar and salt. Spread over the pizza crust. Sprinkle with the goat cheese and figs. Bake at 450 degrees for 15 to 20 minutes or until the crust is golden brown. Serve immediately.

Makes 1 (9-inch) pizza

Focaccia

1 envelope dry yeast
2 cups lukewarm water
1 tablespoon sugar
4 cups flour
2 teaspoons salt
$^1/_4$ cup ($^1/_2$ stick) butter, melted
Chopped fresh rosemary to taste
Rock salt to taste

Dissolve the yeast in the lukewarm water in a bowl. Sprinkle with the sugar. Let stand for 15 minutes. Combine the flour and salt in a bowl and mix well. Stir in the yeast mixture.

Let rise, covered, in a warm place for 30 minutes. Press the dough into a greased 11×13-inch baking pan with greased hands. Let rise, covered, in a warm place for 30 minutes. Drizzle with the butter. Sprinkle with rosemary and rock salt.

Bake at 400 degrees for 20 minutes. Reduce the oven temperature to 300 degrees. Bake for 10 minutes longer. Serve immediately or reheat as needed. You may freeze for future use.

Serves 8 to 10

Chocolate Gelato

$1^1/_2$ cups milk
1 cup cream
4 ounces semisweet chocolate, chopped
$^1/_8$ teaspoon salt
$^1/_2$ cup sugar
4 egg yolks

Combine the milk and cream in a saucepan and mix well. Cook just until heated through, stirring occasionally. Add the chocolate and salt, stirring until the chocolate melts. Whisk the sugar and egg yolks in a bowl until pale yellow. Stir in the chocolate mixture. Return the mixture to the saucepan. Cook over low heat until slightly thickened, whisking constantly. Strain into a bowl. Let stand until cool. Pour into an ice cream freezer container. Freeze using manufacturer's directions or freeze using the alternative method found in the Creamy Lemon Gelato recipe (page 72).

Serves 4

Try these Pizza Toppings:

Grilled Shrimp with Red Pepper Purée and Sweet Onions; Marinated Artichokes, Parmesan Cheese and Feta Cheese; Black Bean Purée, Fajita Chicken, Goat Cheese, and Red Pepper; Roasted Pork with Hoisin Sauce and Chopped Green Onions; Smoked Salmon, Capers, Thinly Sliced Red Onion, and Crème Fraîche; Tapenade with Roasted Garlic and Feta Cheese; Marinated Goat Cheese with Sun-Dried Tomatoes; or Fontina, Parmesan, Mozzarella, and Goat Cheese.

Creamy Lemon Gelato

1^1/$_4$ cups sugar
1 cup water
Juice of 3 lemons
Grated zest of 2 lemons
^{3}/$_4$ cup whipping cream

Combine the sugar, water, lemon juice and lemon zest in a saucepan and mix well. Cook over low heat just until the sugar dissolves, stirring frequently. Let stand until cool. Beat the whipping cream in a mixing bowl until slightly thickened but not firm. Stir in the lemon syrup. Pour into an ice cream freezer container. Freeze using manufacturer's directions.

As an alternative to using an ice cream freezer, pour the mixture into a large stainless steel bowl. Freeze for 10 minutes or until the mixture begins to thicken and become firm. Beat with an electric mixer until light and fluffy. Return to the freezer. Repeat the process 2 or 3 times or until the consistency is light but not necessarily icy.

Serves 4

Vanilla Gelato

2^1/$_2$ cups milk
^{1}/$_2$ cup cream
1 vanilla bean, scraped
4 or 5 egg yolks
^{3}/$_4$ cup sugar

Combine the milk and cream in a saucepan. Cook until reduced by ^{1}/$_2$ cup, stirring frequently. Stir in the vanilla bean scrapings. Remove from heat. Whisk the egg yolks and sugar in a bowl until pale yellow. Stir in the cream mixture. Return the mixture to the saucepan. Cook over low heat until thickened, whisking constantly. Let stand until cool. Pour the mixture into an ice cream freezer container. Freeze using manufacturer's directions or freeze using the alternative method found in the Creamy Lemon Gelato recipe (above). You may substitute 2 teaspoons vanilla extract for the vanilla bean, adding the vanilla extract to the mixture just before chilling.

Serves 4

Chocolate Italian Cream Cake

Cake

2 cups sifted flour
$1/4$ cup baking cocoa
1 teaspoon baking soda
2 cups sugar
$1/2$ cup (1 stick) butter, softened
$1/2$ cup shortening
5 egg yolks
1 cup buttermilk
1 cup shredded coconut
$1/2$ to 1 cup chopped pecans
2 teaspoons vanilla extract
5 egg whites, stiffly beaten

Chocolate Cream Cheese Frosting

1 (1-pound) package confectioners' sugar
$1/4$ cup baking cocoa
8 ounces cream cheese, softened
$1/2$ cup (1 stick) butter, softened
1 teaspoon vanilla extract
Cinnamon (optional)
$1/2$ to 1 cup chopped pecans
Pecan halves

For the cake, sift the flour, baking cocoa and baking soda into a bowl and mix well. Beat the sugar, butter and shortening in a mixing bowl until creamy, scraping the bowl occasionally. Add the egg yolks 1 at a time, beating well after each addition. Add the flour mixture alternately with the buttermilk, beginning and ending with the dry ingredients and mixing well after each addition. Stir in the coconut, pecans and vanilla. Fold in the egg whites. Spoon the batter into 3 greased and floured 8-inch cake pans or a 9×13-inch cake pan. Bake at 325 degrees for 25 to 30 minutes or until the layers test done; cooking time for the rectangular pan will be longer. Cool in pans for 10 minutes. Remove to a wire rack to cool completely.

For the frosting, sift the confectioners' sugar and baking cocoa into a bowl and mix well. Beat the cream cheese and butter in a mixing bowl until creamy. Beat in the vanilla and cinnamon. Add the cocoa mixture gradually, beating constantly until blended. Stir in the chopped pecans. Spread the frosting between the layers and over the top and side of the cake. Arrange the pecans halves in a decorative pattern over the top of the cake.

Serves 12

Toasting and Tasting

From musicals to dramas, pop to opera, contemporary choreography to traditional folk dancing, Austin enjoys a thriving performing arts community. Austin is proud to be one of only fourteen U.S. cities to boast its own ballet, symphony, and opera. Austin plays host to local, regional, national, and international companies among its many theaters, including the Paramount Theatre, the Long Center for Performing Arts, and The University of Texas Performing Arts Center. Zachary Scott Theatre is named for the Austin native who starred in several Hollywood films. Scott's estate, Sweetbrush, is listed on the National Register of Historic Homes.

Menu

Presenting: A Pre-performance Dinner

Appetizers

Smoked Salmon Napoleons
Bacon-Stuffed Cherry Tomatoes
Fromage Blanc Phyllo Cups

Soups

Crab Bisque
Red Bell Pepper Soup with Sambuca Cream

Salads

Goat Cheese Potato Pancakes over Mixed Greens
Sautéed Quail with Dried Cherries
    (pictured at right)

Entrées

Beef Wellington
Crown of Lamb with Spinach and Couscous

Side Dishes

Green Beans with Pecans and Bleu Cheese
Garlic Mashed Potatoes

Desserts

Pears en Croûte
Pecan Lace Baskets
Chocolate Hazelnut Ice Cream
Coffee Cognac Ice Cream
Concord Cake

Canapés, by definition, are small pieces of toasted or untoasted bread that have been cut into various shapes, then garnished with something savory, such as cheese, an herbed spread, or anchovies. A cracker may also be used as the base. Canapés can be formal or casual, hot or cold. They can be served at a luncheon or brunch, or in the evening. The possibilities are endless, but here are a few of our favorites: crème fraîche, smoked salmon, and minced dillweed; mayonnaise, thin lemon slice, red caviar, and parsley; Roquefort butter, thin slice of cucumber, and a walnut; anchovy butter, a small smoked shrimp, and chopped fresh parsley; tapenade, feta cheese, and a small strip of roasted red bell pepper.

Smoked Salmon Napoleons

Pastry
6 sheets phyllo pastry
6 tablespoons butter, melted

Filling
1 cup sour cream
1 cup mascarpone cheese
3 tablespoons chopped capers

Napoleons
16 ounces smoked salmon
1 bunch chives, trimmed, chopped
1 small jar red caviar

For the pastry, unroll the phyllo and cover with waxed paper topped with a damp tea towel to prevent it from drying out. Stack 3 sheets of the phyllo, brushing each layer with some of the butter. Cut the stack lengthwise into four 3-inch strips, then cut into 4 sets vertically for a total of 16 rectangles. Repeat the process with the remaining phyllo and butter. Arrange the rectangles in a single layer on several baking sheets. Bake at 375 degrees for 12 minutes or until light brown. Let stand until cool. You may prepare up to 2 days in advance and store in an airtight container. Reserve the leftovers for another recipe.

For the filling, combine the sour cream, mascarpone cheese and capers in a bowl and mix well. Chill, covered, for up to 2 days to allow the flavors to meld.

For the Napoleons, arrange 1 of the phyllo rectangles on a serving plate. Spread with some of the sour cream mixture and 1 ounce of the smoked salmon. Layer with another phyllo rectangle, sour cream mixture, smoked salmon and phyllo rectangle. Top with a dollop of the sour cream mixture. Sprinkle with the chives and top with 1 scant teaspoon of the caviar. Repeat the process until all of the ingredients are used. Serve immediately.

Serves 8

Crab Bisque

1/2 cup chopped yellow onion
1/2 cup chopped celery
1/4 cup (1/2 stick) butter
1/4 cup flour
4 cups fish stock
1 pound lump white crab meat
2 cups whipping cream
1 teaspoon salt
1/4 teaspoon white pepper
1/8 teaspoon hot pepper sauce

Sauté the onion and celery in the butter in a large saucepan until tender. Add the flour and mix well. Cook until bubbly, stirring constantly. Add the stock gradually, stirring constantly. Simmer for 10 minutes, stirring occasionally.

Stir in the crab meat, whipping cream, salt, white pepper and hot pepper sauce. Cook just until heated through, stirring frequently; do not boil. Ladle into soup bowls.

Avoid excess stirring after adding the crab meat as it tends to cause the crab to break up and become stringy. You may prepare up to 1 day in advance and store, covered, in a glass or porcelain container in the refrigerator. Reheat before serving.

Serves 4

Bacon-Stuffed Cherry Tomatoes

Scoop the pulp from 3 dozen cherry tomatoes, discarding the pulp. Invert onto paper towels to drain. If needed, cut a thin slice from the bottom of each cherry tomato so they will stand upright. Fry 1 1/2 pounds chopped bacon in a skillet until crisp; drain. Combine with 1/3 cup mayonnaise and 8 finely chopped green onions. Stuff the cherry tomatoes with the bacon mixture. Chill, covered, until serving time. Makes 3 dozen.

Red Bell Pepper Soup with Sambuca Cream

Sambuca Cream

1 cup whipping cream
3 tablespoons sambuca
1/2 teaspoon fresh lemon juice

1/4 teaspoon grated lemon zest
1/8 teaspoon sugar

Soup

1/2 cup olive oil
1 cup chopped onion
2 tablespoons minced jalapeño chiles
1 tablespoon dried fennel seeds
1 tablespoon chopped fresh basil
1/2 bay leaf, crumbled
1/2 teaspoon minced garlic
1/4 teaspoon dried thyme
1/2 bay leaf, crumbled
1/4 cup flour

5 cups chicken stock
1/2 cup chopped seeded peeled fresh
    tomato or canned tomato
1 teaspoon tomato paste
6 large red bell peppers, cut into
    2-inch pieces
1/2 to 1 cup heavy cream
1/8 teaspoon sugar
Salt and pepper to taste
Sambuca to taste

For the cream, beat the whipping cream in a mixing bowl until soft peaks form. Add the sambuca, lemon juice, zest and sugar. Beat just until stiff peaks form. Chill, covered, until serving time.

For the soup, heat the olive oil in a large heavy saucepan over medium heat. Stir in the onion, jalapeño chiles, fennel seeds, basil, bay leaf, garlic and thyme. Reduce the heat to low. Cook for 10 to 15 minutes or until the onion is tender, stirring frequently. Stir in the flour. Cook for 10 minutes, stirring constantly.

Bring the stock to a boil in a saucepan. Pour the stock over the onion mixture, stirring constantly to mix. Add the tomato and tomato paste and mix well.

Heat a large skillet coated with nonstick olive oil spray over high heat until hot. Add the bell peppers. Sauté until the skins are blistered and lightly charred. Add the bell peppers to the soup and mix well. Simmer for 20 minutes, stirring occasionally. Remove from heat.

Process the soup in batches in a blender or food processor until puréed. Strain into the saucepan. Bring to a simmer, stirring occasionally. Stir in 1/2 cup of the heavy cream and sugar. Season with salt and pepper. Cook just until heated through, stirring occasionally. Taste and add the remaining 1/2 cup heavy cream if the soup is too spicy. Add a splash of sambuca and mix well. Ladle into soup bowls. Top each serving with a dollop of the Sambuca Cream. You may prepare the soup up to 2 days in advance and store, covered, in the refrigerator. Reheat over low heat, adding the splash of sambuca just before serving.

Serves 6

Goat Cheese Potato Pancakes over Mixed Greens

Vinaigrette

1 tablespoon Spanish sherry vinegar or balsamic vinegar
$1/2$ teaspoon Dijon mustard
Salt and pepper to taste
3 tablespoons virgin olive oil
1 tablespoon minced shallot
1 small garlic clove, minced
2 tablespoons finely sliced fresh chives

Potato Pancakes

1 pound baking potatoes, peeled, coarsely grated
Salt and pepper to taste
1 tablespoon virgin olive oil
4 ounces fresh goat cheese
1 tablespoon finely sliced chives
$1^1/2$ teaspoons virgin olive oil

Salad

4 cups (4 ounces) loosely packed mixed baby lettuce, such as oak leaf, mustard
   greens, Bibb, radicchio, frisée, spinach or arugula
Salt and pepper to taste

For the vinaigrette, whisk the sherry vinegar, Dijon mustard, salt and pepper in a bowl. Whisk in the olive oil, shallot and garlic until emulsified. Stir in the chives. The vinaigrette may be prepared in advance, but use within 1 hour as the garlic flavor tends to become too strong.

For the pancakes, press the excess moisture from the potatoes. Toss the potatoes in a bowl with salt and pepper. Heat 1 tablespoon olive oil in a large skillet over medium-high heat until hot. Spread a $1/4$-inch layer of the potatoes in the skillet, forming a round pancake about $2^1/2$ inches in diameter. Spread $1/4$ of the goat cheese over the potato layer, not quite to the edge. Sprinkle with $1/4$ of the chives. Cover with another thin layer of potatoes, making sure the goat cheese is completely covered. Repeat the process with the remaining potatoes, remaining goat cheese and remaining chives to make 3 more pancakes. Cook for 3 to 4 minutes or until the potatoes are golden brown. Turn the pancakes carefully with a spatula and add $1^1/2$ teaspoons olive oil to the skillet. Cook for 3 minutes longer or until golden brown; drain.

For the salad, toss the mixed lettuce with the vinaigrette in a bowl. Season with salt and pepper if needed. Arrange a mound of the greens in the center of each of 4 serving plates. Top each serving with 1 potato pancake. Serve immediately.

Serves 4

Sautéed Quail with Dried Cherries

Quail

1/2 cup peanut oil
1/2 cup beaujolais or pinot noir
2 tablespoons currant jelly
1 tablespoon soy sauce
2 shallots, sliced

1 sprig of tarragon
Salt and pepper to taste
8 quail, partially boned
2 tablespoons butter
2 tablespoons peanut oil

Cherry Sauce

1 1/2 cups beaujolais
1 cup dried cherries
2 shallots, finely chopped
1/2 cup reduced quail stock

2 tablespoons currant jelly
1 sprig of tarragon, chopped
1/4 cup (1/2 stick) butter
Salt and pepper to taste

Spinach

2 packages fresh spinach, trimmed
3 tablespoons butter

Salt and pepper to taste

For the quail, whisk the peanut oil, beaujolais, jelly, soy sauce, shallots, tarragon, salt and pepper in a stainless steel saucepan. Heat just until warm. Pour over the quail in a shallow dish, turning to coat. Marinate at room temperature for 30 minutes or in the refrigerator for up to 10 hours, turning occasionally; drain. Sauté the quail breast side down in a mixture of the butter and peanut oil in a skillet; turn. Cook for 6 minutes longer or until cooked through. Remove to a heated plate. Cover to keep warm. Discard the pan drippings from the skillet and reserve the skillet to use in the preparation of the sauce.

For the sauce, pour 1/2 cup of the beaujolais into a microwave-safe bowl. Microwave just until warm. Stir in the cherries. Let stand until plump. Deglaze the reserved skillet with the remaining 1 cup beaujolais. Stir in the shallots. Cook until reduced by half, stirring constantly. Stir in the cherries, stock, jelly and tarragon. Cook until reduced by half, stirring constantly. Whisk in the butter. Cook until slightly thickened, stirring constantly. Season with salt and pepper.

For the spinach, sauté the spinach in the butter in a skillet until wilted. Season with salt and pepper.

To assemble, divide the spinach evenly among 4 serving plates. Top each serving with 2 quail. Drizzle with the sauce.

Serves 4

Photograph for this recipe is on page 76.

Beef Wellington

1 (4-pound) beef tenderloin
Flour
3 tablespoons butter
2 cups chopped mushrooms
2 teaspoons chopped fresh chives
$^1/_8$ teaspoon Cognac
4 ounces pâté
Pepper to taste
8 ounces puff pastry
2 egg yolks, beaten

Dust the beef with flour. Sauté the beef in the butter in a skillet just until brown on all sides. Remove to a platter, reserving the pan drippings. Add the mushrooms to the reserved pan drippings. Sauté until tender. Stir in the chives, Cognac and pâté. Let stand until cool.

Make a lengthwise slit $^3/_4$ through the tenderloin to form a pocket. Sprinkle with pepper. Spoon the pâté mixture into the pocket.

Roll the pastry into a thin rectangle on a lightly floured surface. Arrange the tenderloin seam side down on the pastry. Roll to enclose the tenderloin, sealing the ends. Place on a buttered baking sheet. Brush with the egg yolks. Bake at 350 degrees for 30 to 40 minutes or until brown. Let stand for 30 minutes before serving.

Serves 8 to 12

Fromage Blanc Phyllo Cups

Combine 8 ounces fromage blanc or cream cheese, 2 ounces medium goat cheese (Montrachet or feta), 2 eggs, $^1/_4$ cup heavy cream, 2 minced basil leaves, 1 tablespoon hazelnut oil, $^1/_4$ teaspoon dried rosemary, $^1/_8$ teaspoon dried thyme and salt and pepper to taste in a bowl until blended. Spoon into 3 dozen miniature phyllo cups. Bake at 350 degrees until light brown and puffed. Makes 3 dozen.

Crown of Lamb with Spinach and Couscous

2 racks of lamb, trimmed
3 bunches fresh spinach, trimmed, chopped
Lamb stock or water
1 egg
2 tablespoons heavy cream
1 cup Dijon mustard
1 teaspoon salt
6 cups water or stock
2 tablespoons olive oil
1 tablespoon minced shallot
2 cups couscous
Salt and pepper to taste
Sprigs of fresh rosemary
Pink peppercorns

Sear the racks of lamb in a nonstick skillet. Cool slightly. Bring both ends of 1 rack together to form the crown. Tie the two end bones together with kitchen twine. Repeat the process with the other rack. Arrange the crowns upright in a large baking pan.

Toss the spinach with a small amount of lamb stock in a skillet. Cook over high heat until wilted. Remove the spinach to a bowl. Whisk the egg and heavy cream in a bowl until blended. Stir into the spinach. Add the Dijon mustard and 1 teaspoon salt and mix well. Spoon half the spinach mixture into the center of each crown. Cover the ends of the bones with foil to prevent burning. Roast at 350 degrees for 40 minutes.

Combine the water, olive oil and shallot in a 2-quart saucepan. Bring to a boil. Stir in the couscous; reduce heat. Simmer, covered, for 5 to 10 minutes or until tender; stir. Season with salt and pepper to taste.

Spread the couscous on a serving platter. Discard the kitchen twine from the racks. Arrange the 2 racks end to end on the platter so that the tied ends are not exposed. Decorate the tips of the bones with paper frills. Garnish with fresh rosemary and pink peppercorns.

Serves 8

Green Beans with Pecans and Bleu Cheese

4 teaspoons finely chopped shallots
1 tablespoon olive oil
2 teaspoons cider vinegar
$1/2$ teaspoon Dijon mustard
1 tablespoon olive oil
1 cup pecans
Salt to taste
$1^1/2$ pounds fresh green beans
3 ounces bleu cheese
Pepper to taste

Whisk the shallots, 1 tablespoon olive oil, vinegar and Dijon mustard in a bowl. Heat 1 tablespoon olive oil in a skillet over medium-high heat until hot. Add the pecans and salt. Sauté for 1 minute or until the pecans are one shade darker. Drain on a paper towel and coarsely chop.

Blanch the beans in boiling salted water in a saucepan just until tender; drain. Plunge the beans into a bowl of ice water; drain. Combine the beans with the mustard dressing in a salad bowl and toss to coat. Add the cheese and half the pecans and toss gently. Season with salt and pepper. Sprinkle with the remaining pecans. Serve at room temperature.

Serves 4

Roasting Red Bell Peppers

When red bell peppers are in season, buy them! They are very easy to roast, and store very well in the freezer. To roast, cut the bell peppers into halves vertically, discarding the stems and seeds. Arrange cut side down on a greased baking sheet. Broil for 18 to 22 minutes or until blackened. Place in a sealable plastic bag immediately. Let stand until cool. The peels will slip off easily.

Mashed Potatoes

Mash up those cooked potatoes! Turn this traditional side dish into both an entertaining and family favorite by making some exciting new additions. Some of our favorites are: bleu cheese and roasted garlic; roasted garlic and kalamata olives; crisp-cooked bacon and bleu cheese; feta cheese, sun-dried tomatoes, and capers; roasted corn kernels; caramelized onions with crushed red pepper and Parmesan cheese.

Do not overcook potatoes before mashing them. Add enough liquid, such as melted butter, cream, or chicken broth, to moisten. Serve immediately.

Garlic Mashed Potatoes

2 pounds russet potatoes, peeled, cut into $1^{1}/_{2}$-inch pieces
15 garlic cloves
$^3/_4$ cup heavy cream
5 tablespoons unsalted butter
Kosher salt and freshly ground pepper to taste

Combine the potatoes and garlic in a saucepan. Add enough cold water to the saucepan to measure 1 inch. Bring to a boil over high heat; reduce the heat to medium. Cook, covered, for 20 minutes or until the potatoes are tender but not mushy.

Combine the heavy cream and butter in a saucepan. Cook until reduced by $^1/_4$, stirring occasionally. Drain the potato mixture. Spoon into a bowl. Add the hot cream mixture gradually and mash until blended. Season with kosher salt and pepper. Serve immediately or place the covered bowl over a saucepan of simmering water to keep warm.

Try one of these variations for your next dinner party. For Bleu Cheese Mashed Potatoes, omit the garlic and fold in 1 cup of crumbled bleu cheese just before serving. For Green Mashed Potatoes, omit the garlic. Heat the butter in a saucepan until melted. Combine the melted butter with 3 coarsely chopped scallions in a food processor. Process until puréed and stir into the hot heavy cream. Proceed as directed.

Serves 4

Pears en Croûte

Caramel Sauce
1 (14-ounce) can sweetened condensed milk
1 (12-ounce) jar caramel ice cream topping
2 tablespoons lemon juice
1/4 cup Cointreau or other orange-flavor liqueur

Pears
6 ripe pears with stems
2 (15-ounce) packages refrigerated pie pastries
1 egg yolk
1 tablespoon water
Mint leaves

For the sauce, combine the condensed milk and ice cream topping in a saucepan and mix well. Cook until blended and heated through, stirring frequently. Stir in the lemon juice and liqueur. Remove from heat.

For the pears, cut a small slice from the bottom of each pear so the pears will stand upright. Unfold the pie pastry 1 pastry at a time. Roll each pastry into a 10-inch square on a lightly floured surface. Cut each square into 1-inch strips. Starting at the bottom of each pear carefully begin wrapping the pear with 1 pastry strip, overlapping the strip 1/4 inch as you cover the pear. Continue wrapping by moistening the ends of the strips with water and joining to previous strips until the pear is completely covered. Leave a small hole at the top of the pear to place a mint garnish after baking. Arrange the pear on a baking sheet sprayed with nonstick cooking spray. Repeat the process with the remaining pears and remaining pastry.

Whisk the egg yolk and water in a bowl until blended. Brush the pastry with the egg wash. Bake at 350 degrees for 1 hour.

To assemble, spoon 2 to 3 tablespoons of the sauce onto each of 6 dessert plates. Arrange the pears over the sauce. Garnish with fresh mint leaves.

Serves 6

Coffee Cognac Ice Cream

Combine 4 eggs or the equivalent amount of egg substitute, one 12-ounce can evaporated milk, 3/4 cup sugar and 2 1/2 tablespoons espresso powder in a saucepan. Cook over low heat until thickened and of a custard consistency, stirring constantly. Cool slightly. Stir in 1 cup French vanilla coffee creamer and 1/3 cup Cognac. Chill, covered, in the refrigerator. Stir in 1 1/2 cups half-and-half. Process in a blender for several minutes. Pour into an ice cream freezer container. Freeze using manufacturer's directions. Freeze for 24 hours before serving.

Pecan Lace Baskets

1 cup pecans
$^1/_2$ cup blanched almonds
$^1/_2$ cup (1 stick) unsalted butter, melted
$^1/_2$ cup sugar
1 tablespoon light corn syrup
2 tablespoons milk
3 tablespoons bread flour

Combine the pecans and almonds in a food processor. Pulse until mealy. Combine the butter, sugar and corn syrup in a bowl and mix well. Stir in the pecan mixture and milk. Fold in the bread flour. Chill the batter, covered, for 4 hours or until firm.

Flatten two $^1/_4$-cup portions of the batter into 4-inch rounds on a greased baking sheet using a sheet of waxed paper; remove the waxed paper before baking. Bake at 375 degrees for 12 minutes or until caramel colored. Cool just until easily handled.

Cut a short line from the edge of the warm cookies to the centers. Immediately lift each cookie and press into 2 flat-bottomed custard cups to form baskets. Let cool. Remove the baskets from the custard cups. Repeat with the remaining batter. Place 1 of the baskets on each of 8 dessert plates. Spoon Chocolate Hazelnut Ice Cream (below), Coffee Cognac Ice Cream (page 87) or Vanilla Toffee Ice Cream (page 102) into the baskets.

Makes 8 baskets

Chocolate Hazelnut Ice Cream

Egg substitute equivalent to 4 eggs
1 (12-ounce) can evaporated milk
1 cup (6 ounces) semisweet chocolate chips
$^1/_2$ cup sugar
$^1/_2$ cup Nutella chocolate and creamy hazelnut spread
$^1/_2$ cup hazelnut coffee creamer
2 cups half-and-half

Combine the egg substitute, evaporated milk, chocolate chips and sugar in a saucepan. Cook over low heat until thickened and of the consistency of custard, stirring constantly. Cool slightly. Stir in the hazelnut spread and coffee creamer. Chill, covered, in the refrigerator. Stir in the half-and-half. Process in a blender for several minutes. Pour into an ice cream freezer container. Freeze using manufacturer's directions. Freeze for 24 hours before serving.

Serves 4 to 6

Concord Cake

Chocolate Meringue

2 cups plus 2 tablespoons confectioners' sugar
2 tablespoons Ghirardelli baking cocoa
1 cup egg whites, chilled
1/2 cup superfine sugar

Chocolate Mousse Filling

1 cup (2 sticks) butter, chopped, softened
1/2 cup egg yolks, at room temperature
14 ounces Ghirardelli bittersweet chocolate, melted, cooled
6 egg whites, chilled
1/2 cup superfine sugar

For the meringue, sift the confectioners' sugar and baking cocoa into a bowl. Beat the egg whites in a mixing bowl until foamy. Add the sugar gradually, beating until soft peaks form. Beat for 20 minutes or until glossy. Fold in the baking cocoa mixture gently just until mixed. Line 2 flat baking pans with baking parchment. Draw three 8-inch circles on 1 piece of parchment with a pen or pencil. Draw 15 strips 10 inches long on the other. Turn the parchment over so that the ink or lead does not touch the meringue. Fit a pastry bag with a #4 tip. Fill halfway with the meringue. Press the pastry bag from the top and make spirals starting from the center of the circle on the parchment. Work outward, ensuring that each coil touches the previous one. Pipe strips on the remaining parchment. Bake at 200 degrees for 6 to 8 hours. Let stand until cool. Remove gently from the parchment. Store, wrapped in plastic wrap, at room temperature.

For the filling, cream the butter in a mixing bowl for 10 minutes or until light and fluffy, scraping the bowl occasionally. Add the egg yolks and beat until blended. Beat in the chocolate. Beat the egg whites and sugar in a mixing bowl for 5 minutes or until soft peaks form. Lighten the chocolate mixture by folding in 1/4 of the beaten egg whites. Fold the chocolate mixture into the remaining egg whites. Set aside, covered, in a cool place.

To assemble, cut an 8-inch circle from a piece of cardboard. Spread a small amount of the filling in the middle of the circle. Place 1 of the meringues flat side down on the cardboard and gently press to secure. Spread with enough filling to make a layer the same thickness as the meringue, spreading to the edge. Top with another meringue flat side up. Spread with enough filling to make a layer the same thickness as the first filling layer. Top with the remaining meringue flat side up. Trim the edge of the meringues with a serrated knife using the cardboard circle as a guide. Spread the side and top with the remaining filling.

Press the strips of meringue vertically around the side of the cake, touching one another. The strips should be approximately the height of the cake. Break the remaining meringue strips into 1/4-inch pieces and arrange over the top. Sprinkle with additional confectioners' sugar and then with additional baking cocoa. Chill, covered, until serving time.

Serves 12 to 15

An *Austin* state of mind

The Colorado River flows through the heart of Austin and beyond, creating a series of sparkling lakes stretching for more than 100 miles. Lake Austin and Lake Travis attract picnickers, boaters, and every type of water sport enthusiast. Austin's love affair with nature begins with a climb up Mount Bonnell where visitors can savor a violet-tinged sunset over Lake Austin and the panoramic view of the lake and hills. Beautiful weather and an idyllic river setting in the hills make Austin the perfect place for dining al fresco.

Menu

Head outdoors and fire up the grill!

Beverage
   Sea Breeze

Appetizers
   Spicy Glazed Pecans
   Tapenade
   Jalapeño Dove with Monterey Jack

Salads
   Fresh Corn Salad
   Grilled Portobello Mushrooms with
      Balsamic Vinaigrette
   Roasted New Potato Salad
   Spinach Strawberry Salad with
      Goat Cheese Bruschetta

Entrées
   Grilled Pork Tenderloin
   Barbecued Baby Back Pork Ribs with
      Texas Barbecue Sauce
   Grilled Smoked Salmon with
      Tarragon Mayonnaise

Side Dishes
   Grilled Asparagus (pictured at right)
   Skewered Vegetables

Desserts
   Vanilla Toffee Ice Cream
   Chocolate Brownie Ice Cream Sandwiches
   Hazelnut Cookies

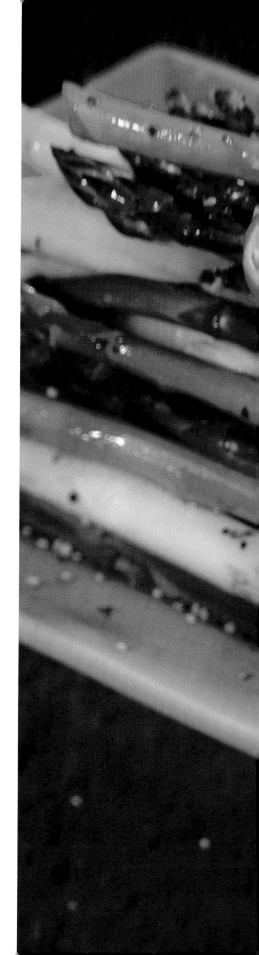

Jalapeño Dove with Monterey Jack

1 cup olive oil
2/3 cup red wine vinegar
3 tablespoons sugar
2 tablespoons Worcestershire sauce
1 teaspoon minced garlic
1 teaspoon salt
Pepper to taste
16 dove breasts, boned
4 jalapeño chiles, seeded, cut into quarters
16 ounces Monterey Jack cheese, cut into 16 slices
8 slices bacon, cut into halves

Combine the olive oil, wine vinegar, sugar, Worcestershire sauce, garlic, salt and pepper in a bowl and mix well. Pour over the doves in a shallow dish, turning to coat. Marinate, covered, in the refrigerator for 24 hours, turning occasionally; drain.

Place 1 jalapeño chile quarter and 1 cheese slice on each dove. Wrap each with 1 bacon half. Secure with wooden picks. Grill the doves over medium-hot coals until the bacon is crisp and the doves are cooked through.

Serves 8

Fresh Corn Salad

8 ears of corn, shucked
1/4 cup water
1 red bell pepper, chopped
1 yellow bell pepper, chopped
1/2 cup thinly sliced green onions with tops
1/2 cup chopped fresh cilantro
1/4 cup each olive oil and lime juice
Juice of 1 orange
1/2 teaspoon each salt and pepper

Remove the corn kernels with a sharp knife into a saucepan. Stir in the water. Steam, covered, for 3 to 5 minutes; remove the cover. Cook for 2 minutes longer or until the liquid is absorbed, stirring constantly. Combine the corn, bell peppers, green onions and cilantro in a bowl and mix well. Whisk the olive oil, lime juice, orange juice, salt and pepper in a bowl. Pour over the corn mixture and toss to coat. Chill, covered, for 2 hours or longer. For variety, grill the corn before removing the kernels.

Serves 4 to 6

Grilled Portobello Mushrooms with Balsamic Vinaigrette

Balsamic Vinaigrette
1 shallot, finely chopped
1 garlic clove, finely chopped
$1/2$ cup extra-virgin olive oil
$1/2$ cup light salad oil
$1/2$ cup balsamic vinegar
Salt and freshly ground pepper to taste

Salad
6 large portobello mushroom caps
Salt and freshly ground pepper to taste
6 to 8 cups salad greens

For the vinaigrette, cook the shallot and garlic in 1 tablespoon of the olive oil in a skillet over low heat until the shallot and garlic are tender, stirring frequently. Remove to a nonreactive bowl with a slotted spoon. Let stand until cool. Stir in the remaining olive oil, salad oil, balsamic vinegar, salt and pepper.

For the salad, sprinkle the mushrooms with salt and pepper. Dip each cap into the vinaigrette until both sides are coated. Arrange the mushrooms top side down on the grill rack. Grill for 4 to 6 minutes. Lift the mushrooms from the grill and rotate each $1/4$ turn halfway through the grilling process to give crisscross grill marks. Turn the mushrooms over. Grill for 4 to 6 minutes longer. Rotate the mushrooms $1/4$ turn again halfway through the grilling process to give the crisscross markings.

Arrange the salad greens on 6 salad plates. Top each plate with a mushroom. Drizzle with the remaining vinaigrette.

Serves 6

Bruschetta comes from the Italian word bruscare, which means to cook over the coals. Slices of Italian bread are rubbed with garlic and brushed with olive oil, then either grilled over coals or broiled in the oven until slightly charred or toasted. Traditional toppings include tomato slices with fresh basil, or mozzarella cheese with tomatoes and basil, but why be traditional? Try a few of the following for a change: goat cheese and roasted portobello mushrooms; basil pesto with roasted red peppers; kalamata olive pesto with roasted garlic cloves; sun-dried tomato pesto with sliced Brie cheese; goat cheese with tomatoes and thinly sliced red onions; or tapenade with goat cheese.

Spicy Glazed Pecans

Heat 2 teaspoons butter in a heavy skillet over medium heat until melted. Stir in 1 tablespoon sugar, 1 teaspoon water, 1/2 teaspoon kosher salt, 1/2 teaspoon black pepper and 1/8 teaspoon cayenne pepper. Cook until bubbly, stirring frequently. Add 2/3 cup pecan halves. Cook for 5 minutes or until the pecans are coated and the sugar has begun to caramelize, stirring constantly. Spread in a single layer on a baking sheet. Let stand until cool. Store in an airtight container. Sprinkle over your favorite salads or serve as an appetizer. Makes 2/3 cup.

Roasted New Potato Salad

Potatoes
2 tablespoons canola oil
1 tablespoon chopped fresh rosemary
1 teaspoon salt
4 pounds unpeeled new red potatoes

Rosemary Mayonnaise
1 tablespoon lemon juice
2 teaspoons Dijon mustard
2 egg yolks or equivalent amount of egg substitute
3/4 cup plus 2 tablespoons canola oil
1 tablespoon chopped fresh rosemary
1/2 teaspoon salt
1/4 teaspoon freshly ground pepper

Salad
1/2 cup chopped scallions (mostly white bulb with 1 to 2 inches of the tops)

For the potatoes, whisk the canola oil, rosemary and salt in a bowl. Add the potatoes and toss to coat. Arrange in a large roasting pan. Roast at 400 degrees for 25 to 40 minutes or until tender. Let stand until cool. Cut the potatoes into quarters.

For the mayonnaise, whisk the lemon juice, Dijon mustard and egg yolks in a bowl until blended. Add the canola oil gradually, whisking constantly until smooth. Add the rosemary, salt and pepper and whisk until combined.

For the salad, toss the potatoes and mayonnaise in a bowl until coated. Add the scallions and mix well. Serve at room temperature.

Serves 8

Spinach Strawberry Salad with Goat Cheese Bruschetta

6 cups (about 1 pound) torn spinach
2 cups strawberry halves
Poppy Seed Dressing (in sidebar)
2 tablespoons slivered almonds, toasted
3 ounces goat cheese, cut into 6 slices
6 slices French bread, toasted

Toss the spinach and strawberries in a bowl. Drizzle with the dressing and mix gently. Spoon 1 cup of the salad onto each of 6 salad plates. Sprinkle each serving with 1 teaspoon of the almonds. Place 1 slice of the cheese on each bread slice. Top each salad with 1 bruschetta.

Serves 6

Grilled Pork Tenderloin

$1/2$ cup soy sauce
$1/2$ cup orange juice
2 tablespoons brown sugar
1 teaspoon ground ginger
2 garlic cloves, crushed
1 ($1^1/2$-pound) pork tenderloin

Combine the soy sauce, orange juice, brown sugar, ginger and garlic in a bowl and mix well. Pour over the tenderloin in a sealable plastic bag and seal tightly. Marinate in the refrigerator for 8 to 10 hours, turning occasionally; drain. Grill the tenderloin over hot coals until a meat thermometer registers 160 degrees. Let stand for several minutes before serving.

Serves 4 to 6

Poppy Seed Dressing

Combine $1/4$ cup sugar, 2 tablespoons sherry or white wine vinegar, $1^1/2$ teaspoons toasted sesame seeds, $1^1/2$ teaspoons olive oil, 1 teaspoon minced red onion, $3/4$ teaspoon poppy seeds, $1/4$ teaspoon Hungarian paprika and $1/8$ teaspoon salt in a jar with a tight-fitting lid and seal tightly. Shake to mix.

Barbecued Baby Back Pork Ribs

Seasoned salt and pepper to taste
8 pounds baby back pork ribs
Texas Barbecue Sauce (below)

Sprinkle seasoned salt and pepper heavily on both sides of the ribs and press lightly. Arrange the ribs in several baking pans. Baste both sides with the barbecue sauce. Pour $1/2$ cup water into the bottom of each pan. Bake at 300 degrees for 2 hours or until almost cooked through, basting frequently with the sauce. Grill over medium to medium-hot coals for 30 minutes or until brown and cooked through, turning and basting frequently with additional sauce. Baking the ribs in the oven first not only cuts down on the grilling time but also helps make the ribs more tender.

Serves 8

Texas Barbecue Sauce

$3/4$ cup cider vinegar
$3/4$ cup warm water
3 tablespoons dry mustard
2 tablespoons dark brown sugar
1 tablespoon salt
1 teaspoon coarsely ground pepper
1 teaspoon paprika
1 teaspoon dark molasses
1 cup (2 sticks) butter
$1/2$ cup ketchup
$1/4$ cup bottled chili sauce
3 tablespoons Worcestershire sauce
2 tablespoons minced onion
1 garlic clove, crushed

Combine the vinegar and warm water in a 2-cup measuring cup. Stir in the dry mustard, brown sugar, salt, pepper, paprika and molasses. Let stand for 10 minutes. Combine the butter, ketchup, chili sauce, Worcestershire sauce, onion and garlic in a saucepan. Bring just to a boil, stirring occasionally. Stir in the vinegar mixture. Reduce the heat to low. Simmer for 30 minutes, stirring occasionally.

Makes 2 to $2^1/2$ cups

Grilled Smoked Salmon with Tarragon Mayonnaise

Chipotle Paste
1 (8-ounce) can chipotle chiles in adobo
4 or 5 garlic cloves, minced
1 tablespoon dried Mexican oregano
2 tablespoons olive oil

Tarragon Mayonnaise
3 egg yolks or equivalent amount of egg substitute
2 tablespoons lemon juice
1 teaspoon Dijon mustard
$^1/_2$ teaspoon salt
$1^1/_2$ cups vegetable or olive oil
1 tablespoon (or more) chopped fresh tarragon

Salmon
8 to 10 salmon fillets
Salt to taste
2 to 4 tablespoons olive oil

For the paste, process the undrained chipotle chiles in a food processor for 1 minute or until puréed. Add the garlic, oregano and olive oil. Pulse just until mixed.

For the mayonnaise, combine the egg yolks, lemon juice, Dijon mustard and salt in a blender. Process until mixed. Add the oil gradually, processing constantly until emulsified. Stir in the tarragon.

For the salmon, brush $^1/_2$ cup of the paste over both sides of the salmon; use the full amount for a very spicy effect and less for a milder flavor. Sprinkle with salt. Brush with the olive oil. Let stand at room temperature for 15 minutes.

Add mesquite chips to hot coals in a grill. Arrange the salmon on the grill rack skin side down when the chips begin to smoke. Cover the salmon with a baking tray or disposable roasting pan to trap the smoke. Smoke for 6 to 7 minutes per side or until the center is just barely cooked and the outside is brown. Serve with the mayonnaise.

Serves 8 to 10

When purchasing fresh asparagus, look at the bud. It should be tightly closed, not open and droopy. Choose asparagus that is bright green in color. The stalk should feel firm and the overall look should be fresh. For grilling, look for asparagus with thick, substantial stalks. For best results, grill the asparagus the same day as purchased. You may store the asparagus for up to 2 days by bunching the asparagus and standing it upright in a glass with 2 inches of cold water. Cover loosely with a plastic bag.

Grilled Asparagus

2 pounds fresh asparagus
1/4 cup extra-virgin olive oil
Salt and freshly ground pepper to taste
2 tablespoons orange juice
1 tablespoon lemon juice

Light the grill, using only hardwood or lump charcoal. The fire is ready in approximately 20 minutes or when the coals glow red and white ash begins to appear on the coals. Spread the charcoal in a single layer to evenly distribute the heat. If you need to add additional coals at any time, arrange them around the rim and they will catch quickly without disturbing the glowing center coals. Set the grill rack 4 inches above the fire and let it heat for 5 minutes. The fire is ready for grilling when you can barely hold your hand 4 inches above the coals for 4 seconds. This is the test for a medium-hot fire.

Trim about 1 inch off the thick woody end of each asparagus spear; the younger and fresher the asparagus, the less you will need to trim from the bottom. Strip away the hard and stringy outer portion of the stalks with a sharp vegetable peeler. Arrange the asparagus in a shallow dish. Drizzle with the olive oil and turn to coat.

Sprinkle salt and a heavier portion of pepper on a plate and mix well. Roll each spear of asparagus in the salt mixture until lightly coated.

Arrange the spears on the grill rack. Grill for 10 minutes or until light brown and of the desired degree of tenderness, turning frequently. Place the asparagus in a shallow serving dish. Drizzle with a mixture of the orange juice and lemon juice. Serve hot or at room temperature. Garnish with strips of orange zest and lemon zest.

Serves 6 to 8

Photograph for this recipe is on page 92.

Skewered Vegetables

Lemon Marinade
1 cup olive oil
$1/4$ cup fresh lemon juice
3 garlic cloves
1 bay leaf

Vegetables
2 red or green bell peppers
3 medium zucchini
18 boiling onions
18 large mushrooms

For the marinade, whisk the olive oil, lemon juice, garlic and bay leaf in a bowl.

For the vegetables, cut the bell peppers into 18 chunks. Cut the zucchini into 18 thick slices. Thread the bell peppers, zucchini, onions and mushrooms alternately on skewers. Arrange the skewers in a single layer in a shallow dish. Drizzle with the marinade, turning to coat.

Marinate at room temperature for 30 minutes; turn. Marinate for 30 minutes longer; drain. Grill the vegetables over hot coals for 10 to 15 minutes or until of the desired degree of crispness.

Serves 6

Tapenade

Use tapenade as a delicious spread, not only for bruschetta but also as a topping for everything from grilled fish to grilled vegetables. Try this recipe for your next cookout. Cut 1 loaf French bread into slices. Arrange on a baking sheet. Toast at 400 degrees until light brown. Combine 1 coarsely chopped oil-pack anchovy fillet and $1 1/2$ tablespoons rinsed coarsely chopped capers in a bowl. Stir in $1/2$ cup finely chopped niçoise olives and $1/2$ cup finely chopped dry-cure black French olives with herbs. Add $1/4$ cup virgin olive oil, 1 small strip of orange zest, $1/4$ teaspoon lemon juice, 1 minced garlic clove and freshly ground pepper and mix well. Spread over 1 side of the toasted bread slices. You may process the tapenade in a blender until puréed for a smoother consistency.

Vanilla Toffee Ice Cream

Combine *4 eggs or equivalent amount of egg substitute, one 12-ounce can evaporated milk and 3/4 cup sugar in a saucepan. Cook over low heat until thickened and of a custard consistency, stirring constantly. Cool slightly. Stir in 1 cup vanilla toffee coffee creamer. Chill, covered, in the refrigerator. Stir in 1 1/2 cups half-and-half. Process in a blender for several minutes. Pour into an ice cream freezer container. Freeze using manufacturer's directions. Stir in 1/2 cup crushed Heath candy bars. Freeze for 24 hours before serving.*

Chocolate Brownie Ice Cream Sandwiches

1/2 cup plus 2 tablespoons flour
1/4 cup baking cocoa
6 ounces semisweet chocolate, melted, warm
1/2 cup (1 stick) unsalted butter, melted
1/4 cup Kahlúa
5 eggs
1 1/4 cups sugar
1 1/4 cups macadamia nuts, chopped
1 cup white chocolate chips or chunks
1 tablespoon espresso powder
4 scoops coffee ice cream
1/2 cup chocolate syrup
Whipped cream
1 tablespoon espresso powder
4 chocolate espresso beans
Confectioners' sugar
Sprigs of mint

Line a 10×15-inch baking pan with foil, allowing a 2-inch overhang. Coat the foil with butter. Sift the flour and baking cocoa into a bowl and mix well. Combine the chocolate, 1/2 cup butter and Kahlúa in a bowl and mix well.

Beat the eggs in a mixing bowl at high speed until frothy. Add the sugar gradually, beating constantly. Beat for 8 to 10 minutes longer or until the mixture is pale yellow and forms a ribbon-like texture. Beat in the chocolate mixture. Fold in the flour mixture in 2 batches. Fold in the macadamia nuts, chocolate chips and 1 tablespoon espresso powder. Spoon the batter into the prepared pan.

Bake at 350 degrees for 20 to 25 minutes or until the brownies test done; do not overbake. Cool in the pan on a wire rack. Cut the brownies into eight 4-inch circles using a round cutter. Arrange 1 brownie circle on each of 4 dessert plates. Spread with ice cream and top with the remaining 4 brownie circles. Drizzle with chocolate syrup. Top with whipped cream, 1 tablespoon espresso powder, espresso beans, confectioners' sugar and sprigs of mint. Serve immediately.

Serves 4

Hazelnut Cookies

12 ounces hazelnuts
$1/4$ cup sugar
6 egg whites, at room temperature
1 cup sugar
$1/8$ teaspoon salt
$1^1/4$ teaspoons vanilla extract, rum or brandy

Spread the hazelnuts in a single layer on a baking sheet. Roast at 350 degrees for 10 minutes or until brown. Cool slightly. Place the warm nuts in batches on a barely damp tea towel. Fold the towel over and rub the hazelnuts vigorously to remove the skins. Let stand until cool. Combine the hazelnuts and $1/4$ cup sugar in a food processor. Pulse until the hazelnuts are ground.

Beat the egg whites in a mixing bowl until frothy. Add 1 cup sugar and salt. Beat until stiff peaks form. Fold in the hazelnut mixture and vanilla until mixed.

Mound by tablespoonfuls $1^1/2$ inches apart on parchment-lined cookie sheets. Bake at 300 degrees for 30 to 40 minutes or until set and brown around the edges. Remove to a wire rack to cool. Serve with Creamy Lemon Gelato (page 72). Bake at 250 degrees for 1 hour for a crisper cookie.

Serves 12

Sea Breeze

Is your fire burning too hot? Cool off with a refreshing Sea Breeze! Fill a glass with ice and pour in two ounces of vodka. Fill the glass with an equal mixture of cranberry juice and grapefruit juice and stir. Don't get too close to the flames! Serves 1.

La Cocina

Alegra

Texas was a part of Spain and then Mexico until it won its independence and became the Republic of Texas. In 1845, it joined the United States of America as the twenty-eighth state. Hispanic culture has influenced Austin and Texas from architecture to language to cuisine. Fiery chiles, traditional tamales, and savory salsas are typical offerings at restaurants. In addition to Mexican restaurants and food markets, Austin boasts Ballet Folklorico, a group of performing artists bringing Hispanic culture to life. The Mexic-Arte Museum features contemporary and historical exhibits focusing on Latino culture.

Menu

La cocina alegra—una fiesta Mexicana!

Beverages
- Blue Margarita
- Traditional Margarita
- Kahlúa

Appetizers
- Ceviche
- Tequila Lime Shrimp
- Corn Dip
- Enchilada Dip
- Guacamole Nuevo
- Shrimp Salsa (pictured at right)
- Jalapeño Fudge
- Poblano and Crab Quesadillas with Tomatillo Mango Relish

Soups
- Cheesy Green Chile Soup
- Santa Fe Gazpacho
- Tomato and Poblano Soup
- Shrimp Enchilada Soup

Salads
- Mango Cabbage Slaw
- Fiesta Chicken Salad with Lime Cilantro Vinaigrette

Entrées
- Grilled Chicken with Mango Salsa
- Tomatillo Chicken Enchiladas
- Sea Bass Habanero

Side Dishes
- Texas Best Black Beans
- Mexican Rice
- Jalapeño Spinach

Desserts
- Chocolate Kahlúa Cheesecake
- South-of-the-Border Bread Pudding
- Mexican Wedding Crescents
- Chocolate Dulces

Ceviche

2 pounds firm white fish, such as orange roughy, chopped
2 cups fresh lime juice
3 firm tomatoes, chopped
1 onion, chopped
1 bell pepper, chopped
1 cup sliced black or green olives
2 tablespoons capers
1 jalapeño chile, chopped
2 tablespoons vegetable oil
1 tablespoon red or white wine vinegar
1 teaspoon Tabasco sauce
Salt and pepper to taste
Garlic powder to taste
Cumin to taste
Chopped fresh cilantro (optional)
Minced garlic (optional)
Sliced avocado
Hearts of palm

Combine the fish and lime juice in a nonmetallic bowl and toss to coat. Marinate, covered, in the refrigerator for 12 to 24 hours, stirring occasionally. Drain and rinse lightly.

Combine the fish, tomatoes, onion, bell pepper, olives, capers and jalapeño chile in a bowl and mix gently. Whisk the oil, wine vinegar, Tabasco sauce, salt, pepper, garlic power, cumin, cilantro and minced garlic in a bowl. Add to the fish mixture and mix gently.

Chill, covered, until serving time or for up to 4 days. Spoon into a serving bowl. Top with avocado slices and hearts of palm. Serve with chips or assorted wheat crackers.

Serves 10 to 12

Tequila Lime Shrimp

2 pounds shrimp
2 cups julienned jicama
1/2 cup vegetable oil
1/4 cup tequila
1/3 cup sugar

1/2 cup chopped fresh cilantro
3 or 4 jalapeño chiles, seeded, finely
  chopped
1 or 2 green onions, thinly sliced

Cover the shrimp with water in a large saucepan. Bring to a boil. Boil until the shrimp turn pink; drain. The cooking time varies according to the size of the shrimp. Boil medium-large shrimp (25 to 30 count) for 4 minutes. Peel and devein the shrimp. Place the shrimp and jicama in a sealable plastic bag.

Whisk the oil and tequila in a bowl. Whisk in the sugar. Stir in the cilantro, jalapeño chiles and green onions. Pour over the shrimp mixture and seal tightly. Marinate in the refrigerator for 2 hours, turning occasionally.

Remove the shrimp from the bag. Pour the remaining marinade onto a platter with sides. Arrange the shrimp over the marinade. Garnish with sprigs of cilantro and additional jalapeño chiles. Serve with wooden picks.

Serves 8

Enchilada Dip

16 ounces reduced-fat cream cheese,
  softened
1 (10-ounce) can diced tomatoes and
  green chiles
4 green onions, chopped
1 bunch cilantro, trimmed, chopped
1 1/2 tablespoons chili powder
1 teaspoon minced garlic

1 teaspoon cumin
1 teaspoon dried oregano
1 teaspoon paprika
Cayenne pepper to taste
Red pepper flakes to taste
3 boneless skinless chicken breasts,
  cooked, chopped
1 1/3 cups shredded Cheddar cheese

Process the cream cheese, undrained tomatoes, green onions, cilantro, chili powder, garlic, cumin, oregano, paprika, cayenne pepper and red pepper flakes in a food processor container until mixed. Spoon into a bowl. Stir in the chicken and Cheddar cheese. Serve with tortilla chips. The flavor is enhanced if the dip is prepared 1 day in advance and stored, covered, in the refrigerator.

Serves 8

Guacamole Nuevo

2 teaspoons unsalted butter
2 teaspoons vegetable oil
3 serrano chiles, cut lengthwise into halves
1 onion, chopped
1¹/₂ tablespoons fresh lemon juice
Salt to taste
3 ripe avocados, pitted, peeled
¹/₂ cup chopped fresh cilantro (optional)

Heat the butter with the oil in a skillet over high heat until melted. Add the serrano chiles and onion. Sauté for 3 to 5 minutes or until light brown. Stir in the lemon juice. Season with salt. Remove from heat.

Remove the chiles carefully to a cutting board and finely chop; the use of rubber gloves is a good idea. Combine the chiles and onion in a mixing bowl or a molcajete. Add the avocados and mash until mixed. Season with salt. Stir in the cilantro. Serve immediately with tortilla chips or serve as a salad or accompaniment.

Chef David Garrido of Jeffrey's contributed this recipe.

Makes 2 cups

Shrimp Salsa

2 pounds boiled shrimp, peeled, deveined
4 or 5 avocados, chopped
8 small tomatoes, chopped
¹/₂ cup chopped fresh cilantro
6 green onions, chopped
2 to 4 jalapeño chiles, seeded, chopped
Juice of 2 limes
1 jar cocktail seafood sauce
¹/₄ cup ketchup
Salt to taste

Combine the shrimp, avocados, tomatoes, cilantro, green onions, jalapeño chiles and lime juice in a bowl and mix gently. Stir in the seafood sauce, ketchup and salt. Chill, covered, until serving time. Garnish with a whole chile. Serve with tortilla chips.

Serves 12 to 15

Photograph for this recipe is on page 106.

Jalapeño Fudge

1 pound Monterey Jack cheese, shredded
1 pound Cheddar cheese, shredded
$1/2$ cup chopped canned jalapeño chiles
$1/2$ cup (or more) chopped green onions
2 eggs
1 cup flour
3 (5-ounce) cans evaporated milk
1 teaspoon cumin
Salt and pepper to taste

Toss the Monterey Jack cheese and Cheddar cheese in a bowl.
Spread in a 9×13-inch baking dish. Sprinkle with the jalapeño chiles and
green onions.

Whisk the eggs in a bowl until blended. Add the flour and whisk
until smooth. Add the evaporated milk gradually, whisking constantly
until blended. Stir in the cumin, salt and pepper.

Pour the egg mixture over the cheese. Bake at 350 degrees for
40 minutes. Let stand until cool. Cut into bite-size squares.

Makes 3 to 4 dozen squares

Tequila

*What goes best with
Mexican food? Cerveza fría (cold
beer) or a margarita. Margaritas
are based on tequila, the most
well-known liquor of Mexico.
True tequila is made from the
blue agave plant, not from the
cactus. Although delicious in the
margarita, well made tequila is
often sipped by itself, like a good
Cognac or brandy.*

Poblano and Crab Quesadillas with Tomatillo Mango Relish

Tomatillo Mango Relish
1 tablespoon olive oil
1 shallot, minced
1 pound tomatillos, husked, cored, cut into quarters
3 or 4 ($1/2$-inch) pieces fresh or canned mango
2 serrano chiles, finely minced (optional)
1 tablespoon chopped fresh cilantro
Salt and white pepper to taste

Quesadillas
$1/4$ cup ($1/2$ stick) unsalted butter
$1/4$ cup olive oil
4 garlic cloves, minced
1 medium onion, finely chopped
1 pound lump crab meat, cartilage removed
4 ounces cream cheese, chopped
2 poblano chiles, roasted, peeled, seeded, finely chopped
3 tablespoons minced fresh cilantro
2 tablespoons mayonnaise
1 teaspoon salt
18 flour tortillas
12 ounces Monterey Jack cheese, shredded

For the relish, heat the olive oil in a skillet until hot. Add the shallot. Cook for 2 minutes or until softened, stirring frequently. Process the tomatillos and mango in a food processor until finely chopped. Add the shallot, serrano chiles, cilantro, salt and white pepper. Process until mixed. Use immediately or store, covered, for up to 1 day in the refrigerator.

For the quesadillas, heat the butter and olive oil in a saucepan until blended. Pour all but 2 tablespoons of the butter mixture into a bowl and set aside. Add the garlic and onion to the remaining 2 tablespoons butter mixture. Sauté over medium heat for 2 minutes. Remove from heat. Stir in the crab meat, cream cheese, poblano chiles, cilantro, mayonnaise and salt.

Spread one side of half the tortillas with the crab meat mixture. Sprinkle with the cheese. Top with the remaining tortillas. Sauté the quesadillas in the reserved butter and olive oil mixture in a large nonstick skillet until brown on both sides. Cut each quesadilla into 6 wedges. Serve with the relish.

You may prepare the quesadillas in advance and brush lightly with the butter and olive oil mixture. Store, covered, in the refrigerator until ready to sauté.

Makes 54 wedges

Cheesy Green Chile Soup

1/2 cup chopped green bell pepper
1/2 cup chopped onion
1/4 cup (1/2 stick) butter
1/3 cup flour
2 (10-ounce) cans chicken broth
4 cups shredded Monterey Jack
   cheese

1 (7-ounce) can chopped green chiles
1/2 teaspoon cumin
1/2 teaspoon dried oregano
1/2 teaspoon cayenne pepper
1 cup half-and-half
Corn tortilla strips

Sauté the bell pepper and onion in the butter in a saucepan over medium-high heat for 3 to 4 minutes or until tender. Add the flour and mix well. Cook for 2 minutes, stirring constantly. Add the broth gradually, stirring constantly.

Cook for 4 minutes, stirring constantly. Reduce the heat to medium-low. Stir in the cheese, green chiles, cumin, oregano and cayenne pepper. Simmer for 10 minutes, stirring frequently. Add the half-and-half and mix well.

Simmer for 5 minutes longer or until heated through, stirring frequently. Ladle into soup bowls. Top with tortilla strips. Serve immediately.

Serves 6

Santa Fe Gazpacho

1 large cucumber, peeled, seeded,
   coarsely chopped
1 (14-ounce) can reduced-sodium
   chicken or vegetable broth
2 tomatoes, cut into quarters
1 (7-ounce) jar roasted red bell
   peppers, drained
3 tablespoons chopped fresh cilantro
2 tablespoons fresh lime juice

2 teaspoons minced canned chipotle
   chiles
Salt and pepper to taste
2 large green onions, finely chopped
1/2 avocado, finely chopped
1/2 cup finely chopped jicama
1/2 cup finely chopped green bell
   pepper
1/2 cup finely chopped plum tomatoes

Combine half the cucumber, 1/2 cup of the broth, 2 tomatoes, roasted red bell peppers, cilantro, lime juice and chipotle chiles in a blender. Process until puréed. Pour into a bowl. Stir in the remaining broth. Season with salt and pepper. Chill, covered, for 2 hours or longer.

Combine 1 heaping teaspoon each of the green onions, avocado, jicama, green bell pepper and plum tomatoes in a bowl and mix gently. Set aside for garnish. Stir the remaining green onions, remaining avocado, remaining jicama, remaining green bell pepper, remaining plum tomatoes and remaining cucumber into the soup. Ladle into chilled soup bowls. Top each serving with some of the garnish.

Serves 4

Traditional Margarita

A margarita is only as good as the ingredients you put into it— use good tequila and fresh lime juice. Combine 1 ounce tequila, 1 ounce fresh lime juice and 1 ounce Cointreau in a cocktail shaker with ice and shake until mixed. Strain into a salt-rimmed glass. Serve immediately with a lime garnish. Serves 1.

Tomato and Poblano Soup

Soup

$1/2$ onion, chopped
2 leeks, chopped
1 poblano chile, roasted, peeled, seeded, chopped
1 rib celery, chopped
5 tomatoes, chopped
$1/2$ cup sherry
1 cup vegetable stock or water
1 cup cream
Salt and pepper to taste
$1/4$ cup tomato purée

Garnish

$1/2$ leek, chopped
$1/2$ poblano chile, roasted, peeled, seeded, chopped
1 tablespoon lemon juice

For the soup, sauté the onion, 2 leeks, 1 poblano chile and celery in a nonstick saucepan until the onion is brown. Stir in the tomatoes. Cook for 5 minutes, stirring occasionally. Add the sherry and mix well.

Cook for 10 minutes or until thickened, stirring occasionally. Stir in the stock. Bring to a boil; reduce heat. Stir in the cream. Simmer for 10 minutes, stirring occasionally. Season with salt and pepper.

Pour the soup into a blender. Process until blended. Strain into the saucepan. Stir in the tomato purée. Cook just until heated through, stirring occasionally. Remove from heat. Cover to keep warm.

For the garnish, sauté $1/2$ leek in a nonstick skillet until tender. Stir in $1/2$ poblano chile and lemon juice. Sauté for 1 minute. Ladle the soup into soup bowls. Top each serving with some of the leek mixture.

Serves 4

Shrimp Enchilada Soup

5 cups chicken broth
4 ounces (3 cups) tortilla chips
2 (4-ounce) cans chopped green chiles
1 (10-ounce) can diced tomatoes and green chiles
2 tablespoons butter or margarine
1 pound medium shrimp, peeled, deveined
1 medium onion, chopped
2 garlic cloves, minced
1 cup sour cream
1/4 cup chopped fresh cilantro
Shredded mozzarella cheese
Shredded Cheddar cheese

Bring the broth to a boil in a large saucepan. Stir in the tortilla chips. Remove from heat. Let stand for 10 minutes. Process the broth mixture in a food processor in 2 batches until smooth, scraping the side once. Return to the saucepan. Stir the green chiles and tomatoes into the broth mixture.

Heat the butter in a skillet over medium-high heat until melted. Add the shrimp, onion and garlic. Cook for 3 to 4 minutes or until the shrimp turn pink, stirring constantly. Stir the shrimp mixture into the broth mixture.

Cook over medium heat until heated through, stirring occasionally; do not boil. Stir in the sour cream and cilantro. Ladle into soup bowls immediately. Sprinkle each serving with mozzarella cheese and Cheddar cheese.

Serves 4 to 6

Blue Margarita

Pour 1 teaspoon kosher salt into a shallow dish large enough to incorporate the rims of the glasses you are using. Rub the rim of each glass with 1 lime wedge. Dip the rim of each glass in the salt and rotate gently to cover the rim evenly. Fill a cocktail shaker halfway with ice. Add 4 ounces tequila, 1/4 cup fresh lime juice, 2 ounces blue curaçao, 1 ounce Triple Sec and 1 teaspoon superfine sugar to the shaker and shake vigorously for 30 seconds. Fill the prepared glasses with ice cubes. Strain the margarita into the glasses. Garnish each with a slice of star fruit or a lime wedge. Makes 2 (6-ounce) drinks.

Mango Cabbage Slaw

1 small head green cabbage, shredded
2 ripe mangoes, chopped
1/2 cup chopped green onions with tops
1 cup plain yogurt
3/4 cup mayonnaise
4 jalapeño chiles, seeded, minced
2 tablespoons Dijon mustard
3 tablespoons sugar
Juice and zest of 1/2 lemon
Salt and freshly ground pepper to taste

Toss the cabbage, mangoes and green onions in a bowl. Whisk the yogurt, mayonnaise, jalapeño chiles, Dijon mustard, sugar, lemon juice, lemon zest, salt and pepper in a bowl.

Add the mayonnaise mixture to the cabbage mixture and toss to coat. Chill, covered, for 1 to 8 hours.

Serves 6

Fiesta Chicken Salad with Lime Cilantro Vinaigrette

Lime Cilantro Vinaigrette
1/2 cup chopped shallots
1/4 cup fresh lime juice
1/4 cup chopped fresh cilantro
1 tablespoon minced garlic
1/2 cup vegetable oil
Salt and pepper to taste

Salad
3 cups thinly sliced red leaf lettuce
3 cups thinly sliced napa cabbage
1 cup chopped cooked chicken breast
2 plum tomatoes, seeded, chopped
1/2 red bell pepper, thinly sliced
1/2 yellow bell pepper, thinly sliced
1/2 avocado, chopped
1/3 cup crumbled tortilla chips
1/4 cup cooked fresh or thawed frozen whole kernel corn
1/4 cup pumpkin seeds or pepitas, toasted
1/4 cup thinly sliced onion
1/2 cup crumbled queso añejo or feta cheese

For the vinaigrette, combine the shallots, lime juice, cilantro and garlic in a bowl and mix well. Whisk in the oil gradually. Season with salt and pepper. You may prepare up to 1 day in advance and store, covered, in the refrigerator. Bring to room temperature before serving.

For the salad, combine the lettuce, cabbage, chicken, tomatoes, bell peppers, avocado, tortilla chips, corn, pumpkin seeds and onion in a bowl and toss to mix. Drizzle with the vinaigrette and mix well. Sprinkle with the cheese.

Serves 6

Grilled Chicken with Mango Salsa

Mango Salsa

6 cups chopped ripe mangoes
1 cup finely chopped red onion
1/2 cup chopped fresh cilantro
6 tablespoons lime juice
2 large garlic cloves, minced
4 jalapeño chiles, seeded, minced
1/2 teaspoon (or more) red pepper flakes
Salt to taste

Chicken

24 small boneless skinless chicken breasts
3/4 cup olive oil
1/2 cup white wine vinegar
3 tablespoons coarsely ground gingerroot
3 tablespoons Dijon mustard
1 tablespoon coriander
1 tablespoon cumin
Freshly ground pepper to taste
Sprigs of cilantro

For the salsa, combine the mangoes, onion, cilantro, lime juice, garlic, jalapeño chiles, red pepper flakes and salt in a bowl and mix well. Chill, covered, in the refrigerator. Bring to room temperature before serving.

For the chicken, arrange the chicken in a nonmetallic dish. Whisk the olive oil, wine vinegar, gingerroot, Dijon mustard, coriander, cumin and pepper in a bowl. Reserve 1/4 cup of the marinade; cover and chill. Pour the remaining marinade over the chicken, turning to coat.

Marinate, covered, in the refrigerator for up to 2 days, turning occasionally; drain. Grill the chicken over medium-hot coals for 6 to 10 minutes or until cooked through, basting with the reserved marinade frequently. Spread the salsa on a serving platter. Top with the chicken and sprigs of cilantro.

Serves 12

Tomatillo Chicken Enchiladas

Tomatillo Sauce

$1/3$ cup vegetable oil
2 medium onions, finely chopped
1 (28-ounce) can tomatillos
2 (4-ounce) cans chopped green
  chiles
1 cup chicken broth

3 tablespoons lime juice
2 teaspoons dried oregano
2 teaspoons sugar
1 teaspoon cumin
Salt to taste

Enchiladas

4 cups coarsely shredded cooked
  chicken or turkey
2 cups shredded Monterey Jack
  cheese
1 or 2 (4-ounce) cans chopped green
  chiles
$1^1/2$ teaspoons dried oregano
Salt and pepper to taste

Vegetable oil
12 to 18 corn tortillas
1 cup shredded Monterey Jack cheese
1 to $1^1/2$ cups sour cream
Chopped fresh cilantro (optional)
Sliced tomatillos (optional)
Lime slices (optional)

For the sauce, heat the oil in a 3- to 4-quart saucepan over medium-high heat until hot. Add the onions. Cook for 10 minutes or until tender, stirring frequently. Stir in the undrained tomatillos, green chiles, broth, lime juice, oregano, sugar and cumin. Bring to a boil, stirring occasionally; reduce heat. Simmer for 25 minutes, stirring occasionally. Process in a blender or food processor until smooth. Season with salt. Return the sauce to the saucepan. Cook just until heated through, stirring frequently. Remove from heat. Cover to keep warm.

For the enchiladas, combine the chicken, 2 cups cheese, green chiles and oregano in a bowl and mix well. Season with salt and pepper.

Add just enough oil to a 10-inch skillet to measure $1/2$ inch. Heat over medium heat until hot. Add 1 tortilla at a time. Cook for 10 seconds or until softened, turning once. Drain on paper towels. Spoon about $1/4$ to $1/2$ cup of the chicken mixture down the center of each tortilla. Roll to enclose the filling. Arrange seam side down in a 9×13-inch baking pan. At this point the enchiladas may be stored, covered, in the refrigerator until the following day.

Bake, covered with foil, at 350 degrees for 15 minutes or until heated through; remove cover. Sprinkle with 1 cup cheese. Bake for 10 minutes longer or until the cheese melts.

Spoon some of the warm sauce onto each of 6 to 9 dinner plates. Arrange 2 enchiladas on each plate. Top with the sour cream. Sprinkle with the cilantro. Arrange the sliced tomatillos and lime slices over the top.

Serves 6 to 9

Sea Bass Habanero

4 (6-ounce) sea bass fillets with skin
Salt and freshly ground pepper to taste
3 tablespoons olive oil
1 small onion, thinly sliced
1 large tomato, seeded, cut into thick strips
1 small mango, chopped
4 garlic cloves, minced
1 habanero chile, seeded, sliced
1/8 teaspoon salt
1/8 teaspoon pepper
1/2 cup dry white wine
1/2 cup clam juice
1/4 cup water
1 lime, cut into 8 wedges
1/4 cup fresh cilantro leaves

Sprinkle the fillets with salt and pepper to taste. Sauté the fillets skin side up in the olive oil in a nonreactive skillet for 1 minute per side or until brown and slightly opaque. Remove to a platter, reserving the pan drippings. Add the onion to the reserved pan drippings. Cook over medium-high heat for 3 minutes or until brown. Increase the heat to high. Add the tomato, mango, garlic, habanero chile, 1/8 teaspoon salt and 1/8 teaspoon pepper.

Cook for 2 minutes or until fragrant, stirring constantly. Stir in the wine. Cook for 2 minutes or until reduced by half, stirring constantly. Stir in a mixture of the clam juice and water. Bring to a boil; reduce heat to medium-low. Simmer for 2 minutes, stirring occasionally.

Squeeze the juice from the lime wedges into the broth and add the wedges and fish. Cook, covered, for 1 to 3 minutes or until the fish flakes easily. Season with salt and pepper to taste. Discard the lime wedges. Spoon the fish and vegetables onto 4 soup plates. Spoon the broth over the top. Sprinkle with the cilantro.

Serves 4

Texas Best Black Beans

1 pound dried black beans
1 onion, minced
3 tablespoons chopped fresh cilantro
2 jalapeño chiles, seeded, finely chopped
1 tablespoon (heaping) chopped garlic
1 teaspoon ground cumin
Salt to taste

Sort the beans. Soak the beans in a generous amount of water in a bowl for 8 to 10 hours. Drain and rinse. Combine the beans, onion, cilantro, jalapeño chiles, garlic and cumin in a large saucepan. Add enough water to cover by $1^1/2$ to 2 inches. Bring to a boil; reduce heat.

Simmer for $2^1/2$ hours or until the beans are tender, stirring occasionally and adding additional water as needed. Season with salt.

Serves 10

Corn Dip

Combine 2 drained 16-ounce cans white Shoe Peg corn, 1 finely chopped tomato, $^1/2$ finely chopped green bell pepper, 3 to 4 tablespoons finely chopped canned jalapeño chiles, 4 to 5 finely chopped green onions, 1 to 2 tablespoons mayonnaise and a generous amount of reduced-sodium lemon pepper in a bowl and mix well. Chill, covered, for 1 hour or longer. Serve with tortilla chips. You may also serve as a salad on a bed of lettuce. Serves 8 to 10.

Mexican Rice

1¹/₂ cups rice
2 tablespoons vegetable oil
2 to 3 tomatoes, chopped
1 onion, chopped
1 jalapeño chile, chopped
2 teaspoons cumin seeds

¹/₂ teaspoon garlic powder
¹/₂ teaspoon pepper
Chopped fresh cilantro to taste
Minced bell pepper to taste
Finely chopped carrots to taste
3 cups boiling salted water

Sauté the rice in the oil in a saucepan until golden brown. Stir in the tomatoes, onion, jalapeño chile, cumin seeds, garlic powder, pepper, cilantro, bell pepper and carrots. Add the boiling salted water and mix well. Reduce the heat to low.

Cook, covered, for 10 to 15 minutes or until the liquid is absorbed and the rice is tender. Remove from heat. Let stand for several minutes before serving. Omit the tomatoes, onion and jalapeño chile and stir in a can of diced tomatoes and green chiles if time is of the essence.

Serves 6 to 8

Jalapeño Spinach

1 tablespoon butter
1 white onion, finely chopped
2 garlic cloves, chopped
1 to 2 jalapeño chiles, chopped
2¹/₂ tablespoons flour
1 cup chicken stock

20 ounces fresh spinach, trimmed,
    torn into bite-size pieces
1 cup cream
8 ounces Cheddar cheese, shredded
1 teaspoon salt
¹/₂ teaspoon pepper

Heat the butter in a sauté pan over medium-high heat until melted. Stir in the onion, garlic and jalapeño chiles. Sauté until the onion is tender. Add the flour and mix well. Stir in the stock. Bring to a boil, stirring frequently.

Add the spinach gradually to the broth mixture, stirring constantly. Cook until the spinach wilts. Stir in the cream. Bring to a boil, stirring frequently; reduce heat. Add the cheese. Cook just until melted, stirring frequently. Stir in the salt and pepper. Spoon into a serving bowl.

Serves 8

Chocolate Kahlúa Cheesecake

Chocolate Crust
1¹/₄ cups graham cracker crumbs
¹/₃ cup butter, melted
¹/₄ cup sugar
¹/₄ cup baking cocoa

Kahlúa Filling
32 ounces cream cheese, softened
1¹/₂ cups sugar
1 cup baking cocoa
4 eggs
¹/₂ cup strong coffee
¹/₂ cup Kahlúa
2 teaspoons vanilla extract

Topping
1 cup sour cream
2 tablespoons sugar
1 teaspoon vanilla extract
6 to 8 chocolate curls (optional)

For the crust, combine the graham cracker crumbs, butter, sugar and baking cocoa in a bowl and mix well. Press the crumb mixture over the bottom of a 9-inch springform pan. Bake at 325 degrees for 5 minutes. Let stand until cool.

For the filling, beat the cream cheese in a mixing bowl until light and fluffy, scraping the bowl occasionally. Add the sugar gradually and beat until blended. Beat in the baking cocoa. Add the eggs 1 at a time, beating well after each addition. Stir in the coffee, Kahlúa and vanilla. Spoon into the prepared pan. Bake at 375 degrees for 50 to 60 minutes or until set.

For the topping, combine the sour cream, sugar and vanilla in a bowl and mix well. Spread over the top of the hot cheesecake. Bake at 425 degrees for 5 to 7 minutes. Cool in the pan on a wire rack to room temperature. Chill, covered, for 8 to 10 hours. Top with the chocolate curls.

Serves 10 to 12

South-of-the-Border Bread Pudding

1 cup sugar
2 cups hot water
2 tablespoons cinnamon
6 slices bread, toasted, cubed
2 cups raisins
2 cups coarsely chopped pecans, toasted
3 cups shredded Monterey Jack cheese

Heat the sugar in a cast-iron skillet until melted and golden brown, stirring constantly. Add the hot water and mix well. Cook until the sugar dissolves, stirring constantly. Stir in the cinnamon. Remove from heat.

Layer the toasted bread, raisins, pecans and cheese $1/2$ at a time in a 2-quart soufflé dish. Pour the sugar mixture over the prepared layers. Bake at 350 degrees for 45 minutes or until the liquid is absorbed.

Serves 6 to 8

Mexican Wedding Crescents

1 cup (2 sticks) butter, softened
$1/3$ cup sugar
4 teaspoons vanilla extract
2 cups flour
1 cup chopped pecans
Confectioners' sugar to taste

Beat the butter and sugar in a mixing bowl until creamy. Add the vanilla and beat until blended. Add the flour and mix well. Stir in the pecans. Shape the dough into a ball. Chill, covered with plastic wrap, until firm.

Shape the dough by tablespoonfuls into crescents or discs on an ungreased cookie sheet. Bake at 325 degrees for 17 to 20 minutes or until brown around the edges. Roll the hot cookies in confectioners' sugar. Cool on a wire rack.

Makes 2 dozen cookies

Chocolate Dulces

2 cups (12 ounces) chocolate chips
$^1/_4$ cup sugar
1 (14-ounce) can sweetened condensed milk
$^1/_2$ cup (1 stick) butter
1 cup flour
1 cup chopped nuts
1 teaspoon Mexican vanilla extract

Combine the chocolate chips and sugar in a double boiler. Cook over hot water until blended, stirring frequently. Add the condensed milk and butter, stirring until blended. Remove from heat. Add the flour, nuts and vanilla and mix well. Let stand for 10 minutes.

Drop the dough by teaspoonfuls onto an ungreased cookie sheet. Bake at 350 degrees for exactly 10 minutes. Remove immediately to a sheet of waxed paper to cool.

Makes 50 cookies

Kahlúa

Kahlúa is a coffee-flavor liqueur traditionally made in Mexico. It is delicious when poured over ice cream, into coffee, or simply sipped alone. It is very easy to prepare at home, and makes a wonderful and well-received gift. Be sure to allow plenty of time to let it mature—it tastes best about thirty days after having been bottled. Combine 2 cups 80 proof vodka, 2 cups water, 1$^1/_4$ cups sugar, 1$^1/_2$ tablespoons vanilla (Mexican vanilla, if you have it) and 1$^1/_2$ tablespoons instant coffee in a saucepan. Cook, covered, over medium heat until the sugar dissolves, stirring occasionally. Remove from heat. Let stand, covered, until cool. Pour into a bottle and seal tightly. Store in a cool dark environment for thirty days.

Putting on the

Ritz

Austin's film industry has exploded over the past decade. With hills to the west, pine trees to the east, and lakes and ranchland all around, it's no wonder that Austin attracts both veteran and novice filmmakers to such a diverse locale. From Hollywood feature films to small independent movies, the Austin area has it all—small towns that time seems to have forgotten . . . city squares and historic courthouses . . . a bustling downtown and bold cityscape.

Menu

Before the Curtain Goes Up:
A sophisticated dinner party before
a movie premiere

Appetizers
Roquefort-Stuffed Endive
Roquefort Walnut Terrine with Apple Relish
Crab Rolls

Soup
Spinach Soup with Crab Meat

Salads
Roquefort and Pear Salad with
  Grapes and Spiced Pecans
Scallop, Orange and Artichoke Salad

Entrées
Pepper-Crusted Beef Tenderloin
Cranberry Pork Tenderloin
Salmon Roulade with Red Pepper Cream

Side Dishes
Green Beans with Orange Sauce
Potatoes with Mushrooms and Brie
Spinach Rockefeller (pictured at right)

Desserts
Mango Peach Sorbet
Chocolate Soufflé Cake
Cream Cheese and Carrot Soufflé

Roquefort-Stuffed Endive

Combine 1/2 cup chopped toasted walnuts or pecans, 1/2 cup crumbled Roquefort cheese and 1/4 cup sour cream in a bowl and mix well. Separate 4 heads endive into spears. Spoon about 1 teaspoon of the cheese mixture onto the stem end of each endive spear. Garnish with edible flowers. Makes 2 dozen.

Roquefort Walnut Terrine with Apple Relish

Roquefort Walnut Terrine

2 cups walnuts
1 pound Roquefort cheese, softened
1 cup crème fraîche or sour cream

Apple Relish

4 medium Granny Smith apples, peeled, thinly sliced
2 tablespoons plus 2 teaspoons fresh lemon juice
1/4 cup olive oil
2 tablespoons Dijon mustard
1 tablespoon plus 1 teaspoon balsamic vinegar
Salt and pepper to taste

For the terrine, spread the walnuts in a single layer on a baking sheet. Toast at 350 degrees for 10 minutes or until light brown, stirring occasionally. Line a 5×7-inch loaf pan with plastic wrap, leaving a 3-inch overhang.

Break up the Roquefort cheese in a bowl with a fork until slightly chunky. Stir in the walnuts and crème fraîche. Spoon into the prepared loaf pan and smooth the top. Cover with the plastic wrap. Chill for 6 to 10 hours.

For the relish, toss the apples with 2 tablespoons of the lemon juice in a bowl. Whisk the remaining 2 teaspoons lemon juice, olive oil, Dijon mustard and balsamic vinegar in a bowl until blended. Season with salt and pepper. Pour over the apples and toss to coat.

To assemble, invert the terrine onto a flat surface and discard the plastic wrap. Run a sharp thin knife under hot water and pat dry. Cut the terrine into 3/4-inch slices with the heated knife. Arrange the slices on a serving platter, rinsing and drying the knife after each cut. Serve with the relish and sliced French bread.

You may substitute pecans for the walnuts, Stilton cheese for the Roquefort cheese and pears for the apples.

Serves 8 to 10

Crab Rolls

20 to 25 slices very thin white bread
8 ounces jalapeño cheese spread
1 cup (2 sticks) butter
1 tablespoon Worcestershire sauce

1 pound lump or claw crab meat
$1/2$ cup (1 stick) butter, melted
$1/2$ cup sesame seeds, toasted

Trim the crusts from the bread. Flatten the slices slightly between sheets of waxed paper with a rolling pin.

Combine the cheese spread and 1 cup butter in a saucepan. Cook over low heat until blended, stirring constantly. Stir in the Worcestershire sauce. Cool slightly. Fold in the crab meat.

Spoon 1 to 2 tablespoons of the crab mixture down 1 edge of each slice of bread. Roll to enclose the filling. Brush the rolls with $1/2$ cup melted butter and coat with the sesame seeds. Cut each roll into halves.

Arrange the rolls in a single layer on a baking sheet. Bake at 375 degrees for 20 minutes or until brown. Serve immediately.

Makes 40 to 50 crab rolls

Spinach Soup with Crab Meat

1 tablespoon virgin olive oil
2 cups chopped onions
1 garlic clove, chopped
1 quart vegetable broth or water
$1/4$ cup finely chopped peeled potato
2 tablespoons shredded coconut
    (optional)

$1/8$ teaspoon sugar
Salt and pepper to taste
1 to $1^1/4$ pounds fresh spinach leaves,
    julienned
8 ounces fresh lump jumbo crab meat
4 teaspoons sour cream
Paprika to taste

Heat the olive oil in a saucepan over medium heat until hot. Add the onions and garlic. Sweat for 6 to 8 minutes or until the onions are tender, stirring frequently. Stir in the broth, potato, coconut, sugar, salt and pepper. Bring to a boil; reduce heat.

Simmer for 10 to 12 minutes, stirring occasionally. Stir in the spinach. Simmer for 3 minutes longer, stirring occasionally. Process the soup in batches in a blender until puréed. Adjust the seasonings. Return the soup to the saucepan. Cook just until heated through, stirring frequently.

Divide the crab meat evenly among 4 heated soup bowls. Ladle the soup over the crab meat. Top each serving with 1 teaspoon of the sour cream and sprinkle with paprika. Serve immediately.

Serves 4

Roquefort and Pear Salad with Grapes and Spiced Pecans

Spiced Pecans
1 tablespoon brown sugar
$1/4$ teaspoon each cayenne pepper and cumin
2 teaspoons vegetable oil
1 cup pecan halves

Apple Walnut Vinaigrette
$1/2$ Granny Smith apple, peeled, chopped
1 shallot
$1/4$ cup vinegar
1 teaspoon sugar
$2/3$ cup corn oil
$1/3$ cup walnut oil
Salt and freshly ground pepper to taste

Salad
$1/2$ small red onion, sliced, separated into rings
8 ounces green beans
Salt to taste
8 ounces each baby mixed greens and seedless red grapes
2 ripe unpeeled pears, cut lengthwise into $1/4$-inch slices
Freshly ground pepper to taste
8 ounces Roquefort cheese
2 tablespoons chopped fresh chives

For the pecans, combine the brown sugar, cayenne pepper and cumin in a bowl and mix well. Stir in the oil. Add the pecans and toss to coat. Spread the pecans in a single layer on a baking sheet. Toast at 350 degrees for 15 to 20 minutes or until light brown, stirring once. Let stand until cool. You may prepare up to 2 days in advance and store in an airtight container.

For the vinaigrette, process the apple and shallot in a blender or food processor until smooth. Add the vinegar and sugar. Process until blended. Add the corn oil and walnut oil gradually, processing constantly until creamy. Season with salt and pepper. Use immediately or store, covered, in the refrigerator. Shake well before using.

For the salad, soak the onion in cold water or wine vinegar in a bowl. Blanch the beans in boiling salted water in a saucepan until tender-crisp; drain. Rinse with cold water until cool; drain. Toss the pecans, drained onion, beans, mixed greens, grapes and pears in a salad bowl. Add half the vinaigrette and toss gently until coated. Sprinkle with salt and pepper. Crumble the cheese over the top and toss to mix. Sprinkle with the chives. Serve with the remaining vinaigrette.

Serves 4 to 6

Scallop, Orange and Artichoke Salad

Balsamic Dressing
1 cup red wine
1/2 cup balsamic vinegar
1 to 2 tablespoons carrot purée
2 tablespoons butter
Salt and pepper to taste

Salad
1 pound sea scallops (8 to 12 per pound)
Virgin olive oil
Salt and pepper to taste
6 cups mixed field greens
1 (14-ounce) can artichoke hearts, drained, outer leaves removed
Sections of 2 oranges

For the dressing, heat the wine in a saucepan until reduced to 1/2 cup. Stir in the balsamic vinegar. Add the carrot purée, butter, salt and pepper. Cook over low heat until blended, stirring frequently. Remove from heat. Let stand until cool.

For the salad, sauté the scallops in olive oil in a skillet over medium-high heat until tender. Season with salt and pepper; drain. Toss the field greens, artichokes and oranges in a bowl. Drizzle with the dressing and toss to coat. Divide the salad evenly among 4 serving plates. Top with the scallops.

Serves 4

Mango Peach Sorbet

Process 2 or 3 peeled mangoes and 1 or 2 peeled peaches in a blender until puréed. Strain, reserving 2 cups. Bring 1/4 cup water and 1/4 cup sugar to a boil in a saucepan. Boil until slightly reduced. Combine the mango and peach purée and 5 to 6 tablespoons of the sugar syrup in a bowl and mix well. Taste and add additional sugar syrup if desired. Stir in 1 tablespoon (more or less) lemon juice and 1 tablespoon (more or less) lime juice. Freeze until of the desired consistency. Serves 4.

Pepper-Crusted Beef Tenderloin

$1/3$ cup cracked peppercorns
Kosher salt to taste
4 (10- to 12-ounce) beef tenderloin
   steaks
3 tablespoons vegetable oil

2 cups port
1 large shallot (2 tablespoons),
   roasted, minced
3 tablespoons honey
3 tablespoons butter

Press the peppercorns and kosher salt into the surface of the steaks. Heat the oil in a large heavy skillet over high heat until hot. Arrange the steaks 2 at a time in the skillet. Cook for 3 minutes per side. Transfer the steaks to a baking sheet, reserving the pan drippings. Bake at 500 degrees for 8 minutes for medium-rare or until of the desired degree of doneness. Let stand for 5 minutes.

Stir the wine into the pan drippings. Cook until reduced by half, stirring occasionally. Add the shallot and honey and mix well. Cook until heated through, stirring frequently. Whisk in the butter until blended. Season with salt. Remove from heat. Cover to keep warm.

Arrange the steaks on 4 dinner plates. Drizzle with the wine sauce. Serve immediately.

Serves 4

Cranberry Pork Tenderloin

$1/3$ cup dried cranberries
$1/2$ to $2/3$ cup dry red wine
Coarsely ground pepper
1 pork tenderloin, cut into 8 tenders

Salt to taste
Olive oil
3 shallots, minced
1 or 2 garlic cloves, minced

Plump the cranberries in the wine in a bowl for 30 minutes to 2 hours, the longer the better. Pat a generous amount of pepper into the tenders and sprinkle with salt. Flatten the tenders between sheets of waxed paper with a meat mallet until doubled in size.

Sauté the tenders in olive oil in a skillet for 2 to 3 minutes per side for medium. Remove to a serving platter with a slotted spoon, reserving the pan drippings. Cover to keep warm. Add the shallots and garlic to the pan drippings.

Sauté for 1 minute. Drain the cranberries, reserving the wine. Add the reserved wine to the shallot mixture. Cook until reduced by $1/3$. Stir in the cranberries. Cook just until heated through, stirring frequently. Drizzle over the tenders.

Serves 4

Salmon Roulade with Red Pepper Cream

Red Pepper Cream

2 red bell peppers, roasted, peeled, seeded
2 cups sour cream
3 tablespoons chopped roasted garlic

Salmon and Assembly

1 (1½-pound) salmon fillet, skin and bones removed
2 bunches leeks, trimmed, chopped
2 tablespoons minced garlic
2 tablespoons butter
1 (10-ounce) package frozen spinach, thawed, drained
⅓ cup dry white wine
Red bell pepper strips
Sprigs of flat-leaf parsley

For the cream, combine the roasted bell peppers, sour cream and garlic in a blender container. Process until smooth.

For the salmon, pound the fillet into a ⅓- to ⅔-inch-thick rectangle between 2 sheets of waxed paper. Sauté the leeks and garlic in the butter in a skillet. Add the spinach and mix well. Stir in the wine. Cook until the liquid is absorbed, stirring frequently.

Spread the spinach mixture over the salmon fillet. Roll to enclose the filling. Wrap the roll in heavy-duty foil. Cook on a griddle or in a large skillet over medium heat for 10 minutes or until of the desired degree of doneness, constantly turning the roll.

To assemble, spoon about 2 tablespoons of the cream onto each of 6 dinner plates. Cut the roulade into 6 or 12 equal portions. Place 1 or 2 portions on each plate. Top with bell pepper strips and sprigs of parsley.

Serves 6

Basic Marinade

Whisk ½ cup orange juice, ½ cup olive, peanut or vegetable oil, ¼ cup barbecue sauce or ketchup, ¼ cup teriyaki sauce, 1 tablespoon Worcestershire sauce, 1 tablespoon honey mustard or honey mustard salad dressing, 1 tablespoon honey or any syrup and 1 tablespoon balsamic vinegar in a bowl. Try one of these optional additions if desired: 1 tablespoon brown sugar, 1 tablespoon chopped garlic, 1 tablespoon chopped gingerroot, 1 teaspoon sesame seeds or ⅛ teaspoon chili powder. Use your imagination. We predict this will become a staple in your kitchen. Use as a marinade for fish, chicken or pork.

Green Beans with Orange Sauce

1 1/2 pounds green beans, trimmed
2 teaspoons butter
1 teaspoon olive oil
1/4 cup chopped green onions
1 garlic clove, minced
1/2 cup orange juice
1/4 cup dry white wine
2 quarts water
Salt to taste
2 tablespoons grated orange zest

Cut the beans lengthwise into halves. Heat the butter and olive oil in a saucepan over low heat until the butter melts. Add the green onions and garlic. Cook for 3 to 4 minutes or until the green onions are tender, stirring constantly. Stir in the orange juice and wine. Sauté over high heat for 4 minutes or until thickened. Remove from heat. Cover to keep warm.

Bring the water and salt to a boil in a saucepan over high heat. Add the beans. Cook for 4 to 5 minutes or until tender-crisp. Drain and pat dry. Place in a serving bowl. Add the orange sauce and toss gently. Sprinkle with the orange zest. Serve immediately.

Serves 4 to 6

Potatoes with Mushrooms and Brie

8 large new potatoes, thinly sliced
1 pound wild mushrooms, sliced
4 shallots, finely chopped
2 tablespoons unsalted butter
1 (1-pound) round Brie cheese, rind removed, cubed
1 1/2 cups whipping cream
6 tablespoons unsalted butter, melted
1/3 cup roasted garlic, mashed
2 tablespoons chopped fresh tarragon

Soak the potatoes in ice water in a bowl for 30 minutes. Drain and pat dry. Sauté the wild mushrooms and shallots in 2 tablespoons butter in a skillet for 10 minutes or until tender. Layer the potatoes, mushroom mixture and Brie cheese 1/3 at a time in a greased baking dish. Whisk the whipping cream, 6 tablespoons melted butter, garlic and tarragon in a bowl until mixed. Pour over the prepared layers. Bake at 375 degrees for 1 to 1 1/4 hours or until the potatoes are tender.

Serves 4 to 6

Spinach Rockefeller

2 (10-ounce) packages frozen spinach
$^3/_4$ cup herb-seasoned stuffing mix
$^1/_2$ cup (1 stick) butter
2 small onions, finely chopped
$^1/_4$ cup grated Parmesan cheese
2 eggs, beaten
1 teaspoon garlic powder
$^1/_8$ teaspoon thyme
Tabasco sauce to taste
6 firm ($^1/_2$-inch-thick) beefsteak tomato slices
$^1/_4$ teaspoon pepper
Salt to taste

Cook the spinach using package directions; drain. Combine the spinach, stuffing mix, butter, onions, cheese, eggs, garlic powder, thyme and Tabasco sauce in a saucepan and mix well. Cook over low heat for 25 minutes, stirring frequently. Remove from heat. Cover to keep warm.

Sprinkle both sides of the tomato slices with the pepper and salt. Arrange in a single layer in a baking dish. Bake at 375 degrees for 10 minutes. Using an ice cream scoop, mound some of the spinach mixture on each tomato slice. May sprinkle additional Parmesan cheese over the top. Serve immediately.

Serves 6

Photograph for this recipe is on page 128.

Chocolate Soufflé Cake

Crème Anglaise

8 egg yolks
$1/2$ cup sugar
1 teaspoon cornstarch
4 cups milk
Seeds from 1 vanilla bean, or 1 teaspoon vanilla extract

Cake and Assembly

7 tablespoons butter
1 cup Ghirardelli semisweet chocolate chips
Grated zest of 1 orange
1 tablespoon vanilla extract
2 tablespoons finely ground almonds
5 egg yolks
9 tablespoons sugar
5 egg whites
Confectioners' sugar

For the crème anglaise, beat the egg yolks and sugar in a mixing bowl until pale yellow and thick. Combine the cornstarch with $1/4$ cup of the milk in a saucepan and mix well. Stir in the remaining milk. Scald the milk, stirring constantly. Add to the egg yolk mixture gradually, whisking constantly. Pour the mixture into a nonaluminum saucepan.

Cook over low to medium heat until a candy thermometer registers 164 degrees or until the mixture begins to coat a wooden spoon, stirring constantly. Strain into a bowl. Stir in the vanilla bean seeds. Let cool to room temperature, stirring occasionally. You may chill, covered with plastic wrap, in the refrigerator.

For the cake, coat the side and bottom of a 10-inch cake pan with butter and dust lightly with flour. Line the bottom with parchment. Combine the butter, chocolate chips, orange zest, vanilla and almonds in a double boiler. Cook over hot water until the butter and chocolate melt, stirring occasionally. Cool to lukewarm.

Beat the egg yolks and $4^1/2$ tablespoons of the sugar in a mixing bowl until pale yellow. Fold in the chocolate mixture. Beat the egg whites in a mixing bowl until foamy. Add the remaining $4^1/2$ tablespoons sugar gradually, beating constantly until stiff peaks form. Fold into the chocolate mixture.

Spoon the batter into the prepared pan. Bake at 275 degrees for 1 hour and 20 minutes. Run a sharp knife around the edge of the pan to loosen the cake. Invert onto a wire rack and again onto a second wire rack so that the cake is right side up. Let stand until cool. The cake will have a crisp sugar crust and the center will sink slightly.

To assemble, sift confectioners' sugar lightly over the top of the cake. Cut into 8 to 12 wedges and arrange on individual dessert plates. Serve with the Crème Anglaise.

Serves 8 to 12

Cream Cheese and Carrot Soufflé

Carrot Cake Batter

$3/4$ cup flour
$1/2$ teaspoon cinnamon
$1/2$ teaspoon freshly grated nutmeg
$1/4$ teaspoon baking soda
$1/8$ teaspoon baking powder
$1/8$ teaspoon salt
2 tablespoons sugar
1 tablespoon brown sugar
1 egg
3 tablespoons vegetable oil
2 tablespoons honey
$2/3$ cup shredded carrots
2 tablespoons chopped pecans, roasted
2 tablespoons raisins

Cream Cheese Soufflé Batter

12 ounces cream cheese
1 cup sugar
6 egg yolks
3 egg whites

Crust

4 sheets phyllo pastry
$1/2$ cup (1 stick) butter, melted

Cream Cheese Sauce

8 ounces cream cheese
$3/4$ cup sugar
1 cup fresh orange juice

For the carrot cake batter, combine the flour, cinnamon, nutmeg, baking soda, baking powder and salt in a bowl and mix well. Beat the sugar, brown sugar and egg in a mixing bowl until of a mousse-like consistency. Add the oil and honey gradually, beating constantly at high speed until blended. Stir in the flour mixture. Add the carrots, pecans and raisins and stir just until mixed.

For the soufflé batter, combine the cream cheese and $1/4$ cup of the sugar in a saucepan. Cook over low heat until blended. Stir in $1/4$ cup of the remaining sugar and 3 of the egg yolks. Cook until thickened, stirring constantly. Let cool. Mix 1 cup of the cooled cream cheese mixture and remaining 3 egg yolks in a bowl. Beat the egg whites in a mixing bowl until soft peaks form. Add the remaining $1/2$ cup sugar gradually, beating constantly for 10 minutes or until stiff peaks form. Fold into the egg yolk mixture.

For the crust, working with one sheet of the pastry at a time, line the bottom and $3/4$ inch up the side of a 9-inch springform pan, brushing with the butter between pastry sheets.

For the cake, spoon the carrot cake batter into the prepared pan. Spread with the soufflé batter. Bake at 350 degrees for 30 minutes. Let stand until cool.

For the sauce, heat the cream cheese and sugar in a saucepan over low heat until blended, stirring constantly. Stir in the orange juice. Cook until blended, stirring constantly. Strain into a bowl.

To serve, cut the soufflé into wedges. Drizzle with the sauce. Garnish with fresh raspberries.

Serves 8 to 12

Don't mess with *Texas*

In Texas, football is a way of life. Austin is fortunate to be the home of The University of Texas Longhorns. Founded in 1883, The University of Texas is the largest single campus institution in the nation and is situated on 357 acres just north of the Texas State Capitol. UT-Austin is home to more than 49,000 students from every county in Texas, all 50 states, and more than 120 foreign countries. While UT boasts national champions and star athletes in numerous men's and women's competitive sports, football season puts sports enthusiasts and socialites all on the same playing field. Fans look forward to each fall with great anticipation of a winning season . . . full of fabulous food.

Menu

Swing down the tailgate and "hook 'em" up with friends old and new!

Appetizers
Mediterranean Goat Cheese Sandwiches
Texas Sushi with Poblano Sauce
Grilled Shrimp Kabobs (pictured at right)
Sun-Dried Tomato Toasts

Salads
Feta, Spinach and Pecan Pasta Salad
Confetti Salad
Tabouli
Wild Rice Salad

Entrées
Beef Tenderloin Stuffed with Goat Cheese
Grilled Pork Tenderloin
Spicy Fried Chicken

Side Dishes
Gingered Broccoli
Southwest Green Chile Corn Bread

Desserts
Cream Cheese Brownies
Chocolate Pecan Bars
White Chocolate Macadamia Nut Cookies

Mediterranean Goat Cheese Sandwiches

1 loaf French bread
2 ounces goat cheese
1 tablespoon olive paste
1 cup trimmed arugula or fresh spinach
4 (^{1}/8-inch-thick) slices red onion, separated into rings
4 (^{1}/8-inch-thick) slices tomato
6 basil leaves, julienned
^{1}/2 teaspoon chopped capers
1 teaspoon balsamic vinegar
^{1}/2 teaspoon olive oil
^{1}/8 teaspoon freshly ground pepper

Slice the loaf lengthwise into halves. Spread the goat cheese over the cut side of the bottom half. Spread the olive paste evenly over the cheese. Layer with the arugula, onion, tomato, basil and capers.

Drizzle the prepared layers with a mixture of the balsamic vinegar and olive oil. Sprinkle with the pepper. Top with the remaining bread half. Cut the loaf diagonally into 4 equal portions. Serve immediately.

Makes 4 sandwiches

Texas Sushi with Poblano Sauce

Poblano Sauce

4 large poblano chiles, roasted, peeled, seeded, chopped
4 cups heavy cream
Chopped fresh cilantro to taste
Salt to taste

Sushi

2 cups drained cooked black beans
2 tablespoons chopped fresh cilantro
1 tablespoon cumin
1 jalapeño chile, chopped
Salt and pepper to taste
12 ounces boneless skinless chicken breasts
1 pound fresh spinach
6 (10-inch) flour tortillas
Vegetable oil
8 ounces jalapeño Jack cheese, cut into $^1/_2$-inch strips
1 red bell pepper, julienned, blanched
1 yellow bell pepper, julienned, blanched
1 carrot, julienned, blanched
1 teaspoon butter, softened

For the sauce, combine the poblano chiles and heavy cream in a saucepan. Cook over low heat until thickened, stirring frequently. Stir in cilantro and salt. Process in a blender or food processor until puréed. Serve at room temperature.

For the sushi, process the beans in a blender or food processor until puréed. Add the cilantro, cumin, jalapeño chile, salt and pepper. Process until blended.

Grill the chicken over hot coals or broil until cooked through. Cool slightly. Cut into strips. Steam the spinach until wilted. Coat the tortillas lightly with oil. Heat the tortillas in a skillet just until softened.

Spread the bean purée $^1/_4$ inch thick over 1 side of each of the tortillas. Arrange the chicken strips over the bean purée. Place a narrow row of the cheese, spinach, red bell pepper strips, yellow bell pepper strips and carrot over the bottom third of each tortilla. Beginning with the filled edge, tightly roll the tortillas to enclose the filling. Seal the edges of the rolls with the butter. Wrap the tortilla rolls individually in plastic wrap. Chill until serving time. Cut each roll into $^3/_4$-inch slices. Serve with the sauce.

Makes 4 dozen

Grilled Shrimp Kabobs

2 pounds (about 3 dozen) jumbo shrimp
1/2 cup olive oil
1/3 cup fresh lime juice
3 tablespoons soy sauce
2 teaspoons chopped fresh gingerroot
1 medium onion, chopped
4 garlic cloves, minced

Peel and devein the shrimp, leaving the tails intact. Combine the olive oil, lime juice, soy sauce, gingerroot, onion and garlic in a bowl and mix well. Pour over the shrimp in a sealable plastic bag and seal tightly. Marinate in the refrigerator for 2 hours, turning occasionally; drain. Thread 3 to 4 shrimp through the tails onto skewers. Grill over medium-hot coals for 3 to 4 minutes per side or until the shrimp turn pink; do not overcook. Serve immediately with grilled corn.

Serves 9 to 12

Photograph for this recipe is on page 142.

Feta, Spinach and Pecan Pasta Salad

8 ounces fresh spinach, trimmed
4 plum tomatoes, chopped
2 teaspoons chopped fresh thyme
6 tablespoons olive oil
Freshly ground pepper to taste
12 ounces penne
2 medium zucchini, julienned
2 tablespoons olive oil (optional)
8 ounces feta cheese, crumbled
1/2 cup pecans, toasted
Salt to taste

Cut the spinach leaves into 1/2x3-inch strips. Combine the spinach, tomatoes, thyme and 6 tablespoons olive oil in a bowl and toss gently to mix. Season with pepper.

Cook the pasta in boiling water in a saucepan for 8 minutes or until al dente. Remove from heat. Stir in the zucchini. Let stand for 15 to 20 seconds. Drain the pasta mixture and rinse with cold water. Add to the spinach mixture and toss to mix. Drizzle with 2 tablespoons olive oil. Add the cheese and pecans and toss to mix. Season with salt. Serve warm or at room temperature.

Serves 4 to 6

Confetti Salad

2 to 3 ears of corn, shucked
2 quarts water
Salt to taste
1 small red bell pepper, julienned
1 small green bell pepper, julienned
2 small yellow squash, sliced
2 small zucchini, diagonally sliced
2 small Japanese eggplant, julienned (optional)
3 or 4 basil leaves, chopped
1 bunch arugula or Bibb lettuce
1 bunch red leaf lettuce, torn
$1/2$ cup rice wine vinegar
$1/2$ cup walnut, olive or cottonseed oil
Pepper to taste

Cook the corn in enough water to cover in a saucepan until tender-crisp; drain. Cool slightly. Remove the kernels of corn with a sharp knife into a bowl. Bring the water and salt to a boil in a saucepan. Add the bell peppers. Parboil for 1 minute or until the color heightens. Remove the bell peppers with a slotted spoon to a bowl of ice water. Let stand until cool; drain. Add the yellow squash, zucchini and eggplant separately to the boiling water, parboiling each for 2 minutes. Remove each vegetable with a slotted spoon to a separate bowl.

Toss the basil, arugula and red leaf lettuce in a bowl. Arrange the greens on a large platter or tray. Whisk the wine vinegar, walnut oil, salt and pepper in a bowl. Add the corn kernels and mix well. Drain, reserving the dressing. Arrange the corn kernels in a spoke pattern to resemble sun rays over the greens, mounding some in the center.

Add the bell peppers, yellow squash, zucchini and eggplant separately to the reserved dressing and toss lightly. Arrange the red, green and yellow vegetables in sections between the corn kernel spokes. Drizzle with any remaining dressing. You may substitute 1 yellow bell pepper cut into wedges for the yellow squash.

Serves 6 to 8

Sun-Dried Tomato Toasts

Rehydrate $1^1/2$ ounces sun-dried tomatoes in boiling water in a heatproof bowl for 5 minutes; drain. Combine the sun-dried tomatoes, $1/4$ cup olive oil, 2 minced garlic cloves, 2 tablespoons minced fresh parsley, 5 chopped basil leaves, 5 chopped scallions, 1 teaspoon freshly ground pepper, $1/2$ teaspoon salt and $1/8$ teaspoon sugar in a bowl and mix well. Chill, covered, for 4 hours. Process in a food processor until smooth. Spread the sun-dried tomato mixture on Spicy Cayenne Toasts (page 27). Sprinkle with 4 ounces crumbled goat cheese. Makes 3 dozen.

Tabouli

2 cups fine bulgur
6 medium tomatoes, chopped
2 bunches parsley, finely chopped
1 cucumber, chopped (optional)
$1/3$ cup chopped red bell pepper
$1/3$ cup chopped green bell pepper
Several sprigs of mint, finely chopped (optional)
$1/2$ to $3/4$ cup vegetable oil
Juice of 4 lemons
2 teaspoons salt

Combine the bulgur with just enough water to cover in a bowl. Let stand for 10 minutes; drain. Press the bulgur to remove any excess moisture. Combine with the tomatoes, parsley, cucumber, bell peppers and mint in a bowl and mix gently. Whisk the oil, lemon juice and salt in a bowl. Add to the bulgur mixture and mix until coated. You may serve immediately but the flavor is enhanced if the tabouli is prepared 1 day in advance and stored, covered, in the refrigerator.

Serves 6 to 8

Wild Rice Salad

8 ounces wild rice
1 cup dried cranberries
1 cup pecan pieces
$1/2$ cup orange juice
Grated zest of 1 orange
4 green onions, sliced
$1/4$ cup extra-virgin olive oil
$1^1/2$ teaspoons salt
Freshly ground pepper to taste

Cook the wild rice using package directions. Let stand until room temperature. Combine the wild rice, cranberries, pecans, orange juice, orange zest, green onions, olive oil, salt and pepper in a bowl and mix well. The flavor is enhanced if the salad is prepared in advance and stored, covered, in the refrigerator. Bring to room temperature before serving.

Serves 4 to 6

Beef Tenderloin Stuffed with Goat Cheese

1 (12-ounce) beef tenderloin or beef loin roast
5 ounces goat cheese
3/4 cup packed fresh spinach leaves
2 garlic cloves, minced
1 teaspoon salt
1 teaspoon pepper (optional)
2 tablespoons black peppercorns, coarsely crushed

Cut a slit in the tenderloin to form a pocket. Combine the goat cheese, spinach, garlic, salt and pepper in a bowl and mix well. Spoon the goat cheese mixture into the pocket. Secure at 1- to 2-inch intervals with kitchen twine. Pat the peppercorns over the surface of the tenderloin and press lightly.

Arrange the tenderloin in a shallow roasting pan. Roast at 425 degrees for 15 minutes. Reduce the oven temperature to 325 degrees. Roast for 45 minutes longer or until a meat thermometer registers 135 degrees. Let rest for several minutes. Discard the kitchen twine. Cut the tenderloin into slices of the desired thickness.

Serves 2 to 4

Grilled Pork Tenderloin

1/4 cup sesame oil
1/3 cup soy sauce
1/3 cup packed brown sugar
2 tablespoons Worcestershire sauce
2 tablespoons lemon juice
4 garlic cloves, crushed
1 tablespoon dry mustard
1 1/2 teaspoons pepper
1 (1 1/2- to 2-pound) pork tenderloin

Whisk the sesame oil, soy sauce, brown sugar, Worcestershire sauce, lemon juice, garlic, dry mustard and pepper in a bowl. Pour over the pork in a shallow dish, turning to coat. Marinate, covered, in the refrigerator for 2 hours, turning occasionally; drain.

Place the pork on a grill rack 6 inches from the coals. Grill over medium-hot coals for 30 to 40 minutes or until a meat thermometer registers 160 degrees for medium or 170 degrees for well-done. You may roast the pork in the oven at 300 to 400 degrees for 30 to 40 minutes.

Serves 6

Spicy Fried Chicken

2 (3-pound) chickens
1 quart buttermilk
1 teaspoon freshly ground black pepper
$1/2$ teaspoon cayenne pepper
$1/2$ teaspoon salt
4 garlic cloves, slightly crushed
3 cups unbleached flour
2 teaspoons salt
2 teaspoons freshly ground black pepper
2 teaspoons cayenne pepper
1 teaspoon paprika
Vegetable oil for frying

Cut each chicken into 8 pieces. Whisk the buttermilk, 1 teaspoon black pepper, $1/2$ teaspoon cayenne pepper, $1/2$ teaspoon salt and garlic in a large bowl and mix well. Add the chicken, turning to coat. Chill, covered, in the refrigerator for 8 to 10 hours, stirring once or twice; drain.

Combine the flour, 2 teaspoons salt, 2 teaspoons black pepper, 2 teaspoons cayenne pepper and paprika in a shallow dish and mix well. Coat the chicken with the flour mixture and shake off excess. Arrange the chicken in a single layer on a baking sheet. Let stand for 30 minutes.

Pour enough oil into a large heavy skillet to measure $1/2$ inch. Heat to 360 degrees. Coat the chicken with the flour mixture again. Add 4 to 6 chicken pieces 1 piece at a time to the hot oil in order to maintain a temperature of 320 degrees during the frying process. Fry for 10 to 15 minutes or until cooked through and golden brown on all sides; drain.

Serves 8

Gingered Broccoli

Florets of 2 pounds broccoli, cut into bite-size pieces
2 tablespoons toasted sesame oil
2 large garlic cloves, minced
$1/4$ cup reduced-sodium chicken stock or broth
2 tablespoons reduced-sodium soy sauce
2 tablespoons chopped candied ginger
Salt and freshly ground pepper to taste
4 green onions, chopped

Sauté the broccoli in the sesame oil in a skillet until deep green. Add the garlic. Sauté for 30 seconds. Remove from heat. Stir in the stock, soy sauce and ginger. Spoon into a bowl. Chill, covered, in the refrigerator.

Let the broccoli stand until room temperature. Reheat, covered, in a saucepan over low heat or microwave in a microwave-safe dish. Season with salt and pepper. Spoon the broccoli into a serving bowl. Sprinkle with the green onions. Serve immediately.

Serves 6 to 8

Southwest Green Chile Corn Bread

1 cup (2 sticks) butter, softened
$3/4$ cup sugar
4 eggs
1 cup flour
1 cup yellow cornmeal
2 tablespoons baking powder
1 teaspoon salt
$1^1/2$ cups cream-style corn
$1/2$ cup chopped green chiles
$1/2$ cup shredded Cheddar cheese
$1/2$ cup shredded Monterey Jack cheese

Beat the butter and sugar in a mixing bowl until creamy. Add the eggs 1 at a time, beating well after each addition. Stir in a mixture of the flour, cornmeal, baking powder and salt. Add the corn, green chiles and cheese and mix well. Spoon into a buttered 9×9-inch baking pan. Bake at 325 degrees for 50 minutes.

Serves 9

Cream Cheese Brownies

Brownies

1¹/₃ cups butter
8 ounces semisweet chocolate
³/₄ cup chocolate chips
2 tablespoons water
¹/₂ cup confectioners' sugar
2 teaspoons vanilla extract
2 cups sugar
1¹/₂ cups flour
³/₄ teaspoon salt
¹/₄ teaspoon baking soda
6 eggs, beaten
2 cups chopped nuts

Cream Cheese Topping

16 ounces cream cheese, softened
1 cup sugar
4 eggs
¹/₄ cup (¹/₂ stick) butter
2 teaspoons vanilla extract

Chocolate Glaze

1 cup (6 ounces) chocolate chips
2 tablespoons butter
2 tablespoons water
2 tablespoons corn syrup

For the brownies, combine the butter, semisweet chocolate, chocolate chips and water in a double boiler. Cook over hot water until blended, stirring frequently. Add the confectioners' sugar and vanilla, stirring until blended. Remove from heat. Cool slightly.

Combine the sugar, flour, salt and baking soda in a bowl and mix well. Stir in the eggs. Add the nuts and mix well. Combine with the chocolate mixture and mix well. Spread the batter in a 9×13-inch baking pan sprayed with nonstick cooking spray.

For the topping, beat the cream cheese, sugar, eggs, butter and vanilla in a mixing bowl until smooth. Spread over the prepared layer. Bake at 350 degrees for 30 minutes or until the edges pull from the sides of the pan.

For the glaze, combine the chocolate chips, butter, water and corn syrup in a saucepan. Cook over medium-low heat until blended, stirring frequently. Drizzle over the hot baked layer. Let stand until cool. Cut into bars.

Makes 15 brownies

Chocolate Pecan Bars

2 cups flour
2 cups packed brown sugar
$^1/_2$ cup (1 stick) plus $1^1/_3$ cups ($2^2/_3$ sticks) butter, softened
1 cup pecan halves
1 cup (6 ounces) chocolate chips

Combine the flour, 1 cup of the brown sugar and $^1/_2$ cup of the butter in a mixing bowl. Beat at medium speed until crumbly. Press the crumb mixture over the bottom of a 9×13-inch baking pan. Pierce the prepared layer with a fork. Arrange the pecans over the top.

Combine the remaining 1 cup brown sugar and remaining $1^1/_3$ cups butter in a saucepan. Bring to a boil over medium heat, stirring constantly. Boil for 1 minute, stirring constantly. Drizzle over the prepared layers. Bake at 350 degrees for 18 to 22 minutes or until bubbly. Remove from oven. Sprinkle with the chocolate chips. Let stand for 2 to 3 minutes or until soft; swirl over the top. Cool in the pan on a wire rack. Cut into bars. Do not substitute margarine for butter in this recipe.

Makes 3 dozen bars

White Chocolate Macadamia Nut Cookies

2 cups flour
1 teaspoon baking soda
$^1/_2$ teaspoon salt
$^3/_4$ cup ($1^1/_2$ sticks) unsalted butter, softened
1 cup packed brown sugar
$^3/_4$ cup sugar
2 eggs
1 teaspoon vanilla extract
12 ounces white chocolate, chopped
$1^1/_2$ cups macadamia nuts, chopped

Sift the flour, baking soda and salt together. Beat the butter in a mixing bowl until creamy. Add the brown sugar and sugar gradually, beating constantly until light and fluffy. Add the eggs 1 at a time, beating well after each addition. Beat in the vanilla. Stir in the white chocolate and macadamia nuts with a wooden spoon.

Drop by teaspoonfuls onto a nonstick cookie sheet. Bake at 300 degrees for 14 minutes or until light brown. Cool on the cookie sheet for 2 minutes. Remove to a wire rack to cool completely.

Makes 4 dozen cookies

Great
Beginnings

Sweet Endings

The Austin Museum of Art offers exhibits at
its downtown location and at beautiful Laguna
Gloria, a 1916 Mediterranean-style villa situated
on twelve acres on the banks of Lake Austin.
The Harry Ransom Humanities Research Center
includes the Gutenberg Bible and the world's
first photograph among its permanent collection.
The George Washington Carver Museum was the
first African American neighborhood museum
in Texas. Its collection preserves artifacts that
document the history of African Americans in
the United States. The Jack Blanton Museum of
Art features old masters as well as contemporary
exhibits. Indian artifacts, dinosaur tracks, and
the original Goddess of Liberty are displayed in
the Texas Memorial Museum on The University
of Texas campus. Austin boasts more artists per
capita than any other Texas city and is home to
more than thirty art galleries and museums.

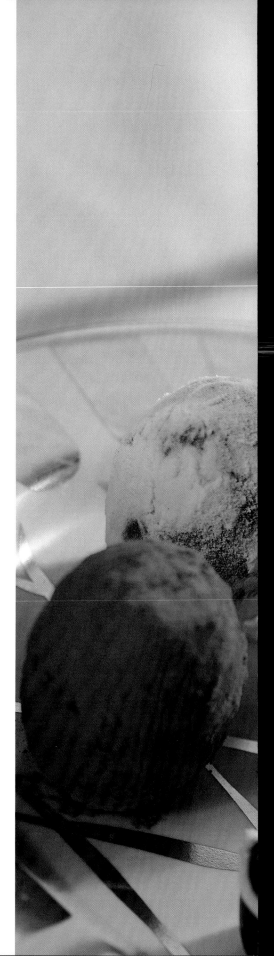

Menu

Celebrate the art of the Dessert!

Beverage
Bellini

Desserts
Turtle Cheesecake
Fallen Chocolate Soufflé Cake
Chocolate Fudge Terrine with Crème Anglaise
   and Raspberry Purée
Rum and Brown Sugar Peaches
Frozen Lemon Soufflé
Sour Cherry Carrot Cake
Carrot Cake
Lady Orange Cake
Peach Torte Cake
Chewy Pecan Pralines
Chocolate Truffles (pictured at right)
Key Lime Pie with
   Shortbread Macadamia Crust
Cranberry Orange Tart

Turtle Cheesecake

Crust
2 cups chocolate wafer crumbs
$1/3$ cup butter, melted
$1/4$ cup sugar

Cream Cheese Filling
24 ounces cream cheese, softened
$1^1/4$ cups sugar
4 eggs
1 cup sour cream
1 tablespoon vanilla extract

Chocolate Topping
$1/4$ cup ($1/2$ stick) butter
1 cup (6 ounces) semisweet chocolate chips
1 (12-ounce) jar caramel ice cream topping
1 cup chopped pecans

For the crust, combine the chocolate wafer crumbs, butter and sugar in a bowl and mix well. Press the crumb mixture over the bottom and 1 inch up the side of a lightly greased 9-inch springform pan. Bake at 325 degrees for 10 minutes. Cool in the pan on a wire rack.

For the filling, beat the cream cheese in a mixing bowl until creamy. Add the sugar gradually, beating constantly until blended. Add the eggs 1 at a time, beating well after each addition and scraping the side of the bowl as needed. Stir in the sour cream and vanilla. Spoon into the prepared crust. Bake at 325 degrees for 65 minutes; the center will not be completely set. Turn off the oven.

Let the cheesecake stand in the oven with the door ajar for 1 hour. Remove to a wire rack to cool completely. Chill, covered, for 8 hours or longer. Remove the side of the pan carefully and place the cheesecake on a serving plate.

For the topping, heat the butter in a saucepan until melted. Stir in the chocolate chips. Cook over low heat until blended, stirring frequently. Spread over the top of the cheesecake. Chill for 15 minutes. Combine the caramel topping and pecans in a saucepan. Bring to a boil over medium heat, stirring constantly. Boil for 2 minutes. Remove from heat. Cool for 5 minutes. Spread over the top of the cheesecake. Let stand until cool. Serve immediately or store, covered, in the refrigerator.

Serves 12

Fallen Chocolate Soufflé Cake

1 pound semisweet chocolate, chopped
1 cup (2 sticks) unsalted butter
9 egg yolks
$1/2$ cup sugar
9 egg whites
1 teaspoon sugar
3 tablespoons sifted baking cocoa
3 tablespoons sifted confectioners' sugar
1 cup whipping cream, whipped

Coat the side and bottom of a 9-inch springform pan with butter and dust lightly with flour. Line the bottom with parchment paper. Butter and flour the parchment paper.

Heat the chocolate and 1 cup butter in a double boiler over low heat until blended, stirring constantly. Remove from heat. Let stand until cool. Beat the egg yolks and $1/2$ cup sugar in a mixing bowl until the mixture is pale yellow and slightly thickened. Beat the egg whites and 1 teaspoon sugar in a mixing bowl until soft peaks form.

Fold together $1/3$ of the chocolate mixture and $1/3$ of the egg yolk mixture in a bowl. Fold in $1/3$ of the beaten egg whites. Repeat the process until all 3 mixtures are incorporated. Spoon the batter into the prepared pan. Bake at 300 degrees for 30 minutes; do not overbake. The center of the cake will not be set. Cool in the pan on a wire rack for 3 hours.

Dust the top of the cake with 1 tablespoon of the baking cocoa and 1 tablespoon of the confectioners' sugar in the order listed. Repeat the process once. Chill, covered, for 8 to 10 hours. Let the cake stand at room temperature for 1 hour. Dust with the remaining 1 tablespoon baking cocoa and remaining 1 tablespoon confectioners' sugar. Remove the side of the pan carefully and place the cake on a cake plate. Slice the cake into 12 wedges with a heated knife. Top each serving with whipped cream.

Serves 12

Bellini

This festive drink is always a way to make your occasion more joyous. Process 1 fresh peach or $1/2$ cup canned peaches in a blender until puréed. Spoon 1 ounce or about 1 tablespoon of the purée into each glass. Fill with Champagne. Cheers! Purée the peaches in advance and store in the refrigerator to eliminate the sound of the blender during your party. Serves 1 or 2.

Chocolate Fudge Terrine with Crème Anglaise and Raspberry Purée

1^1/$_2$ pounds semisweet chocolate, chopped
6 egg yolks
1 cup (2 sticks) butter, softened
9 egg whites, at room temperature
^{1}/$_2$ cup sugar
1 cup chopped pecans
Crème Anglaise (page 138)
Raspberry purée

Heat the chocolate in a double boiler over simmering water until melted, stirring frequently. Pour into a bowl. Let stand until cool. Whisk the egg yolks in a double boiler over simmering water for 2 minutes or until thick and pale yellow. Remove from heat. Whisk until completely cool.

Beat the butter in a mixing bowl until light and fluffy. Fold in the chocolate. Fold in the egg yolks. Beat the egg whites in a mixing bowl until soft peaks form. Add the sugar 1 tablespoon at a time, beating constantly until stiff glossy peaks form. Fold into the chocolate mixture. Spoon into a buttered 5×9-inch loaf pan. Sprinkle with the pecans and press lightly. Chill, covered, for 3 hours or until set.

Let stand at room temperature just until slightly softened. Cut into 8 thin slices. Serve with Crème Anglaise and raspberry purée.

Serves 8

Rum and Brown Sugar Peaches

Peaches
3 pounds ripe peaches
Lemon juice
$1/4$ cup packed dark brown sugar
$1/4$ cup dark rum

Topping and Assembly
1 cup sour cream
1 cup whipping cream
Mint leaves
Fresh raspberries
Grated chocolate

For the peaches, peel the peaches and slice into a bowl. Drizzle with lemon juice. Add the brown sugar and dark rum and toss lightly. Chill, covered with plastic wrap, for 4 hours or longer.

For the topping, spoon the sour cream into a medium bowl. Beat the whipping cream in a mixing bowl until soft peaks form. Fold the whipped cream into the sour cream. Chill, covered, until serving time.

To assemble, spoon the peaches into 8 dessert bowls or goblets. Spoon the topping over the peaches. Top with mint leaves, raspberries and grated chocolate.

Serves 8

Fromage is simply the French word for cheese. A cheese course is traditionally served at the end of a meal in France, and the practice is spreading throughout the United States. A cheese tray is a wonderful way to give your guests an alternative to a sweet for a dessert. Make sure that you select a variety of cheeses: some sharp and some mild, some hard and some semisoft or soft.

Frozen Lemon Soufflé

Crust
1 cup flour
1/2 cup (1 stick) butter, softened
2 tablespoons confectioners' sugar

Lemon Filling
5 egg yolks
1/2 cup sugar
1/2 cup lemon juice
2 teaspoons grated lemon zest
5 egg whites
1/2 cup sugar
2 cups whipping cream, whipped

For the crust, combine the flour, butter and confectioners' sugar in a food processor. Process until crumbly. Press the crumb mixture into a greased 9-inch springform pan. Bake at 425 degrees for 8 to 10 minutes or until light brown. Let stand until cool.

For the filling, combine the egg yolks, 1/2 cup sugar, lemon juice and lemon zest in a double boiler. Cook over simmering water until thickened, stirring constantly. Remove from heat. Let stand until cool.

Beat the egg whites in a mixing bowl until soft peaks form. Add 1/2 cup sugar. Beat for 1 minute longer. Fold the egg whites and whipped cream into the lemon mixture. Spoon into the prepared pan. Freeze, covered, for 2 hours or longer. Garnish with lemon zest and fresh raspberries.

Serves 12

Sour Cherry Carrot Cake

Cake

2 cups flour
1 tablespoon minced fresh gingerroot
2 teaspoons baking soda
2 teaspoons cinnamon
1 teaspoon grated fresh nutmeg
$1/2$ teaspoon salt
$1^{1}/_{2}$ cups sugar
1 cup chopped fresh or canned mango

$3/4$ cup mayonnaise
3 eggs, lightly beaten
$1/4$ cup fresh or canned mango juice
1 cup julienned peeled carrots
1 cup julienned peeled jicama
1 cup dried sour cherries
1 cup pecan pieces

Sour Cherry Cream Cheese Frosting

$1/2$ cup heavy cream
$1/2$ cup dried sour cherries
1 tablespoon vanilla extract
1 tablespoon Jamaican dark rum

1 cup (2 sticks) butter, softened
8 ounces cream cheese, softened
1 (1-pound) package confectioners'
   sugar

For the cake, combine the flour, gingerroot, baking soda, cinnamon, nutmeg and salt in a bowl and mix well. Whisk the sugar, mango, mayonnaise, eggs and mango juice in a bowl. Stir into the flour mixture. Fold in the carrots, jicama, sour cherries and pecans.

Spoon the batter into 2 greased and floured 10-inch cake pans. Bake at 350 degrees for 50 to 55 minutes or until the layers test done. Cool in the pans for 10 minutes. Remove to a wire rack to cool completely.

For the frosting, heat the heavy cream and dried sour cherries in a saucepan over medium-low heat for 7 minutes or until the cherries are plump, stirring occasionally. Let stand until cool. Combine the cherry mixture, vanilla and rum in a blender or food processor. Process until smooth.

Beat the butter and cream cheese in a mixing bowl until creamy, scraping the bowl occasionally. Add the cherry mixture and mix well. Add the confectioners' sugar gradually, beating constantly until of a spreading consistency. Spread the frosting between the layers and over the top and side of the cake.

Chefs Jeff Blank and Jay Moore of Hudson's-on-the-Bend contributed this recipe.

Serves 12

Carrot Cake

Pecan Cream Filling

1¹/₂ cups sugar
¹/₄ cup flour
1¹/₂ cups heavy cream

³/₄ cup (1¹/₂ sticks) unsalted butter
1¹/₄ cups chopped pecans
2 teaspoons vanilla extract

Cake

2 cups flour
2 teaspoons cinnamon
2 teaspoons baking powder
1 teaspoon baking soda
1 teaspoon salt
2 cups sugar

1¹/₄ cups corn oil
4 eggs
4 cups (about 1 pound) grated
   carrots
1 cup chopped pecans
1 cup raisins

Cream Cheese Frosting

8 ounces unsalted butter, softened
8 ounces cream cheese, softened
1 (1-pound) package confectioners'
   sugar, sifted

1 teaspoon vanilla extract
4 ounces flaked coconut, toasted

For the filling, combine the sugar and flour in a saucepan and mix well. Add the heavy cream gradually, stirring constantly. Add the butter. Cook over low heat until the butter melts, stirring constantly. Simmer for 20 to 30 minutes or until golden brown, stirring occasionally. Cool to lukewarm. Stir in the pecans and vanilla. Let stand until cool. Chill, covered, for 8 to 10 hours. Bring to room temperature before using if too thick to spread.

For the cake, sift the flour, cinnamon, baking powder, baking soda and salt into a bowl and mix well. Whisk the sugar and corn oil in a bowl. Sift half the flour mixture into the sugar mixture and mix well. Alternately sift in the remaining flour mixture while adding the eggs 1 at a time, mixing well after each addition. Stir in the carrots, pecans and raisins. Spoon into a greased and floured 10-inch tube pan. Bake at 350 degrees for 70 minutes. Cool upright in the pan on a wire rack. Remove the cake from the pan, wrap in plastic wrap and store at room temperature if not assembling.

For the frosting, beat the butter in a mixing bowl until creamy. Add the cream cheese. Beat until blended. Add the confectioners' sugar and vanilla and beat until of a spreading consistency. Chill if needed for a better spreading consistency. Chill, covered, if not using immediately.

To assemble, run a sharp knife around the edge of the cake. Invert onto a serving plate. Split the cake horizontally into 3 layers with a serrated knife. Spread the filling between the layers. Spread the frosting over the side and top of the cake. Pat the coconut over the side of the cake. If desired, reserve ¹/₂ cup of the frosting and color half with green food coloring and half with orange food coloring. Decorate the top of the cake with green and orange carrots. Serve at room temperature.

Serves 16 to 20

Lady Orange Cake

Cake
2 cups flour
1 teaspoon baking soda
$1/2$ teaspoon salt
2 cups sugar
1 cup (2 sticks) butter, softened
4 eggs
$1^1/3$ cups buttermilk
2 cups flour
1 cup chopped dates
1 cup chopped pecans
1 tablespoon grated orange zest

Orange Glaze
1 (1-pound) package confectioners' sugar
Juice of 4 oranges

For the cake, combine 2 cups flour, baking soda and salt in a bowl and mix well. Beat the sugar and butter in a mixing bowl until creamy, scraping the bowl occasionally. Add the eggs 1 at a time, beating well after each addition. Add the flour mixture alternately with the buttermilk, mixing well after each addition.

Combine 2 cups flour, dates, pecans and orange zest in a bowl and mix until coated. Fold into the batter. Spoon the batter into a 10-inch greased and floured tube pan. Bake at 350 degrees for $1^1/4$ hours.

For the glaze, whisk the confectioners' sugar and orange juice in a bowl. Drizzle over the hot cake until no more of the glaze can be absorbed. Let stand until cool. Remove the cake to a serving plate. Drizzle the remaining glaze over the cake.

Serves 16

Peach Torte Cake

Cake

1 cup flour
2 teaspoons baking powder
$1/2$ teaspoon salt
$1/2$ cup (1 stick) butter, softened
$1/2$ cup sugar
4 egg yolks
1 teaspoon vanilla extract
5 tablespoons milk
4 egg whites
1 cup sugar
1 teaspoon vanilla extract
$3/4$ cup chopped nuts

Filling and Assembly

2 cups whipping cream
2 (16-ounce) cans sliced peaches, drained

For the cake, line two 10-inch springform pans with waxed paper; grease and dust lightly with flour. Combine the flour, baking powder and salt in a bowl and mix well. Beat the butter and $1/2$ cup sugar in a mixing bowl until creamy, scraping the bowl occasionally. Add the egg yolks and 1 teaspoon vanilla and beat until blended. Beat in the flour mixture and milk until smooth. Spoon the batter into the prepared pans.

Beat the egg whites in a mixing bowl until soft peaks form. Add 1 cup sugar gradually, beating constantly until stiff peaks form. Fold in 1 teaspoon vanilla. Spread over the prepared layers. Sprinkle with the nuts. Bake at 350 degrees for 25 minutes. Cool in the pans on a wire rack.

For the filling, beat the whipping cream in a mixing bowl until stiff peaks form. Arrange 1 cake layer meringue side down on a serving platter. Spread with the whipped cream. Fan the peaches over the whipped cream. Top with the remaining cake layer meringue side up. Chill, covered, for 4 to 6 hours before serving. You may prepare up to 1 day in advance and store, covered, in the refrigerator.

Serves 12

Chewy Pecan Pralines

2 cups sugar
2 cups light corn syrup
2 cups (4 sticks) unsalted butter
2 cups whipping cream
2 teaspoons vanilla extract
7 cups pecan pieces or halves

Heat the sugar and corn syrup in a saucepan until a candy thermometer registers 245 degrees, stirring frequently. Remove from heat. Stir in the butter. Add the whipping cream gradually, stirring constantly. Return to heat. Cook for 45 to 60 minutes or until a candy thermometer registers 242 degrees, stirring constantly. Remove from heat. Stir in the vanilla and pecans. Drop by spoonfuls onto buttered foil. Let stand until cool. Wrap the pralines individually in plastic wrap.

Makes 3 dozen large pralines or 5 dozen small pralines

Chocolate Truffles

2 cups heavy cream
$1/4$ cup sugar
1 pound semisweet or bittersweet chocolate, melted
$1/2$ cup (1 stick) butter, softened
1 teaspoon vanilla extract
Baking cocoa
Shredded coconut
Toasted chopped hazelnuts or pecans
Confectioners' sugar

Heat the heavy cream and sugar in a saucepan over low heat until the sugar dissolves, stirring frequently. Remove from heat. Stir in the chocolate. Add the butter and mix well. Stir in the vanilla. Spoon into a bowl. Let stand until room temperature. Chill, covered, for 2 to 3 hours. Using a small melon baller, shape the chocolate mixture into balls. Arrange the truffles on a baking sheet lined with waxed paper. Chill for 30 minutes or longer. Roll the truffles in baking cocoa, shredded coconut, toasted hazelnuts, confectioners' sugar and/or decorate with icing.

Makes 3 dozen truffles

Photograph for this recipe is on page 156.

Key Lime Pie with Shortbread Macadamia Crust

Shortbread Macadamia Crust
1 cup crushed shortbread cookies
5 tablespoons unsalted butter, melted
1/4 cup sugar
1/2 cup finely chopped macadamia nuts

Pie
1 (14-ounce) can sweetened condensed milk
4 egg yolks or equivalent amount of egg substitute
8 ounces cream cheese, softened
2 tablespoons grated Key lime zest
1/2 cup Key lime juice or fresh lime juice
1 cup whipped cream, whipped
10 macadamia nuts, coarsely chopped

For the crust, combine the cookie crumbs, butter, sugar and macadamia nuts in a bowl and mix well. Press into a 9-inch pie plate. Freeze until firm.

For the pie, combine the condensed milk and egg yolks in a food processor. Process until blended. Add the cream cheese and Key lime zest. Process until smooth. Add the lime juice gradually, processing constantly until blended. Spoon into the prepared pie plate. Chill, covered, for 8 to 10 hours. Spread with the whipped cream and sprinkle with the macadamia nuts.

For variety, pipe the whipped cream into 1-inch mounds along the edge of the pie. Place a lime twist and a macadamia nut on top of each mound.

Serves 6 to 8

Cranberry Orange Tart

1 cup slivered almonds
$1/2$ cup (1 stick) butter, chopped
1 cup flour
3 tablespoons brown sugar
1 egg
$1/2$ cup flour
1 envelope unflavored gelatin
$1/4$ cup cold water
$1/4$ cup orange juice
$2/3$ cup orange marmalade
$1/2$ to $3/4$ cup packed brown sugar
$41/2$ cups fresh or frozen cranberries
$1/3$ cup orange marmalade

Process the almonds in a food processor until ground. Add the butter, 1 cup flour, 3 tablespoons brown sugar and egg. Process until the mixture forms a ball. Add $1/2$ cup flour. Process until the mixture forms a ball. Press the dough over the bottom and 2 inches up the side of a 9-inch springform pan. Chill for 20 minutes. Bake at 350 degrees for 20 to 25 minutes or until the edge is golden brown. Let stand until cool.

Soften the gelatin in the cold water in a bowl. Combine the gelatin mixture and orange juice in a saucepan and mix well. Cook until the gelatin dissolves, stirring constantly. Stir in $2/3$ cup marmalade and $1/2$ to $3/4$ cup brown sugar. Bring to a boil, stirring frequently. Stir in the cranberries. Reduce the heat to simmer.

Simmer, covered, for 10 minutes, stirring occasionally. Remove from heat; skim off the foam. Spoon over the baked layer. Chill, covered, for 2 to 10 hours. Remove the side of the pan and place the tart on a serving platter. Heat $1/3$ cup marmalade in a saucepan and brush over the top of the tart.

Serves 12

Wild about
Wildflowers

In spring, the bluebonnets, redbuds, and
peach trees blossom, draping Austin in a
colorful mosaic of pastels. Zilker Botanical
Gardens provide an oasis of inspiration,
beauty, and tranquility amidst its flowers,
shrubs, trees, and ponds. The Umlauf
Sculpture Garden and Museum integrates
sculptures by internationally renowned artist
Charles Umlauf with a Xeriscaped garden.
The Lady Bird Johnson Wildflower Center
combines research and education while
showcasing native plant species with
landscaping. A garden is the ideal setting for
an elegant afternoon entertaining friends.

Menu

*Celebrate spring's arrival with
flowers and friends!*

Beverage
Mint Tea

Soup
Minted Green Pea and Spinach Soup

Salads
Fresh Fruit Toss
Mushrooms with Asparagus and Greens
Seafood Pasta Salad
Wild Tuna Salad

Entrées
Spinach-Stuffed Chicken Breasts in Puff Pastry
Molasses-Glazed Salmon with
   Black Mustard Seed Vinaigrette
Sauté of Soft-Shell Crabs with Wilted Spinach and
   Warm Tomato Vinaigrette
Crab Strudel
Swiss Tarts (pictured at right)

Side Dish
Artichoke Bottoms with Spinach Stuffing

Desserts
Lime Mousse
Frozen White Chocolate Terrine
Chocolate Raspberry Cake à la Simca

Minted Green Pea and Spinach Soup

1 (10-ounce) package frozen spinach, thawed, drained
4 teaspoons unsalted butter
2 cups finely chopped yellow onions
3 cups chicken stock
1 (10-ounce) package frozen green peas, thawed, drained
2 cups loosely packed fresh mint
1 cup heavy cream
Salt and freshly ground pepper to taste

Press the excess moisture from the spinach. Heat the butter in a large saucepan over low heat until melted. Add the onions. Cook for 25 minutes or until tender, stirring occasionally. Stir in the stock. Add the spinach and peas and mix well. Bring to a boil; reduce heat.

Simmer, partially covered, for 20 minutes or until the peas are tender, stirring occasionally. Add the mint. Simmer for 5 minutes. Strain, reserving the liquid. Purée the vegetable mixture in a food processor or blender with 1 cup of the reserved liquid. Return the purée to the saucepan. Add 1 cup of the reserved liquid and heavy cream and mix well. Cook just until heated through, adding additional reserved liquid as needed for the desired consistency and stirring frequently. Season with salt and pepper. Ladle into soup bowls.

Serves 4 to 6

Fresh Fruit Toss

1 pint fresh strawberries
1 cup fresh blueberries
1 cup fresh raspberries
Sections of 2 oranges
3 kiwifruit, sliced
1 small cantaloupe, chopped
1 cup fresh pineapple chunks
1/2 cup fresh orange juice
2 bananas, sliced
Sprigs of fresh mint

Combine the strawberries, blueberries, raspberries, orange sections, kiwifruit, cantaloupe and pineapple in a salad bowl and mix gently. Add the orange juice and toss to coat. Chill, covered, until serving time. Add the bananas and mix gently. Garnish with the mint.

Serves 8

Mushrooms with Asparagus and Greens

1 cup olive oil
$1/2$ cup balsamic vinegar
1 tablespoon chopped fresh basil
1 teaspoon minced garlic
1 teaspoon chopped shallot
$1/8$ teaspoon salt
$1/8$ teaspoon pepper
16 fresh shiitake mushrooms, stems removed
20 spears fresh asparagus, cut into 5-inch pieces
6 cups mixed salad greens
1 cup chopped red tomato
1 egg yolk or equivalent amount of egg substitute

Whisk the olive oil, balsamic vinegar, basil, garlic, shallot, salt and pepper in a bowl until mixed. Add the mushrooms and toss to coat. Marinate at room temperature for 1 hour or longer. The mushrooms will absorb the vinegar before the oil. Do not refrigerate; refrigeration could cause the oil to solidify, preventing the marinade from being absorbed.

Blanch the asparagus in boiling water in a saucepan. Plunge the asparagus into a bowl of ice water. Let stand until cool; drain.

Arrange the salad greens on the bottom half of each of 4 serving plates. Fan the asparagus over the chopped tomato on the top halves of the plates. Drain the mushrooms, reserving the marinade. Arrange the mushrooms in the center of the plates overlapping the asparagus and salad greens.

Whisk the egg yolk into the reserved marinade, adding additional balsamic vinegar if needed. Drizzle over the salad.

Serves 4

Wild Tuna Salad

Cook one 6-ounce package long grain and wild rice using package directions. Combine the rice, one 12-ounce can drained water-pack tuna, 1/2 cup sour cream, 1/2 cup chopped celery, 1/4 cup chopped green bell pepper, 1 tablespoon chopped onion, 1/8 teaspoon salt and 1/8 teaspoon pepper in a bowl and mix well. Chill, covered, until serving time. Spoon onto a lettuce-lined serving platter. Sprinkle with 1 cup salted cashews. Use as an entrée or as a spread on your favorite bread. Serves 6.

Seafood Pasta Salad

3 quarts water
2 tablespoons salt
8 ounces small shell pasta
1 tablespoon vegetable oil
4 hard-cooked eggs
1/2 cup mayonnaise
1/2 cup mayonnaise-type salad dressing
1/3 cup chili sauce
1/4 cup sour cream
1 tablespoon lemon juice
1/2 teaspoon salt
2 (6-ounce) packages crab meat
2 pounds shrimp, boiled, chilled, peeled, deveined
1/3 cup chopped celery
1/3 cup chopped broccoli, lightly steamed
1/4 cup sliced green onions with 1 inch of tops
Leaf lettuce
Sliced tomatoes (optional)
Sliced avocados (optional)

Bring the water and 2 tablespoons salt to a boil in a saucepan. Add the pasta. Boil until al dente. Drain and rinse twice with cold water. Combine the pasta and oil in a bowl and toss to coat. Chill, covered, in the refrigerator.

Chop 2 of the hard-cooked eggs and the whites of the remaining 2 eggs, reserving 2 of the egg yolks. Combine the chopped eggs, chopped egg whites, mayonnaise, salad dressing, chili sauce, sour cream, lemon juice and 1/2 teaspoon salt in a bowl and mix well. Add the mayonnaise mixture, crab meat, shrimp, celery, broccoli and green onions to the pasta mixture and toss to mix. Chill, covered, for 3 hours or longer.

Spoon the salad onto lettuce-lined salad plates. Grate the reserved egg yolks over the top of each serving. Arrange tomato and avocado slices around each serving.

Serves 4 to 6

Spinach-Stuffed Chicken Breasts in Puff Pastry

4 boneless skinless chicken breasts
$1/2$ teaspoon salt
$1/2$ teaspoon pepper
1 (10-ounce) package frozen chopped spinach, thawed, drained
1 cup finely chopped prosciutto
$3/4$ cup grated Gruyère cheese
$1/4$ teaspoon salt
$1/8$ teaspoon pepper
$1/8$ teaspoon nutmeg
1 (17-ounce) package puff pastry
1 egg, beaten
1 teaspoon water
1 recipe Hollandaise Sauce (see page 190)

Pound the chicken between sheets of plastic wrap with a meat mallet until flattened. Sprinkle with $1/2$ teaspoon salt and $1/2$ teaspoon pepper.

Press the excess moisture from the spinach. Combine the spinach, prosciutto, cheese, $1/4$ teaspoon salt, $1/8$ teaspoon pepper and nutmeg in a bowl and mix well. Divide the spinach mixture into 4 equal portions. Mound 1 portion in the center of each chicken breast. Fold the chicken over the filling to cover.

Roll each sheet of pastry on a lightly floured surface into a 12-inch square. Cut a 1-inch strip off the short end of each sheet for the garnish. Cut each pastry sheet vertically into 2 squares. Arrange each chicken breast in the center of a pastry square. Fold the pastry over to enclose, pressing the edges to seal. Brush the seams with a mixture of the egg and water to seal. Arrange seam side down in a greased baking pan.

Cut the reserved pastry into decorative designs and arrange over the top of each packet. Chill for 1 hour. Bake at 400 degrees for 20 to 40 minutes or until the chicken is cooked through and the pastry is brown. Serve with the Hollandaise Sauce. You may substitute veal for the chicken.

Serves 4

Molasses-Glazed Salmon with Black Mustard Seed Vinaigrette

Black Mustard Seed Vinaigrette

$^1/_4$ cup malt vinegar
3 tablespoons honey
2 tablespoons black mustard seeds
1 tablespoon molasses
1 tablespoon light brown sugar
$^3/_4$ cup olive oil

Salmon and Assembly

$^1/_2$ cup molasses
$^1/_4$ cup Dijon mustard
2 tablespoons malt vinegar
$1^1/_2$ teaspoons chopped shallots
1 garlic clove, minced
$^1/_2$ teaspoon pepper
6 (6- to 7-ounce) salmon fillets
6 to 8 cups mixed salad greens

For the vinaigrette, whisk the malt vinegar, honey, black mustard seeds, molasses and brown sugar in a bowl. Add the olive oil gradually, whisking constantly until mixed. You may prepare the vinaigrette up to 1 day in advance and store, covered, at room temperature. Whisk before serving.

For the salmon, combine the molasses, Dijon mustard, malt vinegar, shallots, garlic and pepper in a bowl and mix well. Pour over the salmon in a sealable plastic bag and seal tightly. Marinate in the refrigerator for 3 to 4 hours, turning occasionally; drain. Grill over hot coals or broil for 5 minutes per side or just until cooked through. Remove to a platter. Cover with foil to keep warm.

To assemble, toss the greens in a bowl with just enough of the vinaigrette to coat. Arrange the greens evenly on 6 serving plates. Top each serving with a salmon fillet. Drizzle with the remaining vinaigrette.

Serves 6

Sauté of Soft-Shell Crabs with Wilted Spinach and Warm Tomato Vinaigrette

Warm Tomato Vinaigrette
3/4 cup extra-virgin olive oil
2 tablespoons balsamic vinegar
Juice of 1 small lemon
1 cup each yellow pear tomato halves and red cherry tomato halves
1 red tomato, chopped
1 yellow tomato, chopped
1/4 cup fresh basil, cut into chiffonade strips
1 shallot, minced
Salt and pepper to taste

Spinach
2 garlic cloves, chopped
1/4 cup extra-virgin olive oil
2 pounds fresh baby leaf spinach, trimmed
2 tablespoons water
Salt and pepper to taste

Crabs
6 soft-shell crabs, eyes and gills removed
1 cup skim milk
3/4 cup flour
6 tablespoons each unsalted butter and olive oil

For the vinaigrette, whisk the olive oil, balsamic vinegar and lemon juice in a nonreactive saucepan. Stir in the tomatoes, basil and shallot. Season with salt and pepper. Simmer over low heat until heated through, stirring occasionally. Remove from heat. Cover to keep warm.

For the spinach, sauté the garlic in the olive oil in a sauté pan over medium heat. Add the spinach, water, salt and pepper and toss to coat. Cook just until the spinach wilts, stirring frequently. Remove from heat. Cover to keep warm.

For the crabs, soak the crabs in the milk in a bowl for 5 minutes; drain. Coat the crabs with the flour, shaking off the excess. Heat the butter and olive oil in a large skillet over high heat until hot. Add the crabs. Sauté for 6 to 8 minutes or until crisp and reddish brown, turning halfway through the sautéing process; drain. Arrange on a serving platter. Cover to keep warm.

To assemble, divide the spinach evenly among 6 plates. Place 1 soft-shell crab beside each mound of spinach. Spoon the vinaigrette around the spinach and crabs.

Serves 6

Soft-Shell Crabs

What a delicacy! Soft-shell crabs are crabs in the molting process. Between mid-May and late September, blue crabs shed their hard shells. For about two days, the new shell is very tender and thin and totally edible, and their bodies are very clean since they stop eating two to three days before the molting begins. They truly taste delicious, and, by the way, you do eat the whole thing!

Crab Strudel

1 tablespoon lemon juice
8 ounces crab meat, cartilage and shell removed
2 tablespoons minced scallions
1 tablespoon butter
2 tablespoons chopped fresh parsley
2 drops of Tabasco sauce
$1/8$ teaspoon salt
$1/8$ teaspoon freshly ground pepper
8 ounces Brie cheese, cut into thin strips
6 sheets frozen phyllo pastry, thawed
2 tablespoons butter, melted

Drizzle the lemon juice over the crab meat in a bowl. Sauté the scallions in 1 tablespoon butter in a skillet. Stir in the crab meat. Cook until heated through, stirring constantly. Add the parsley, Tabasco sauce, salt and pepper and mix well. Arrange the Brie cheese slices over the top of the crab meat mixture. Cook until the cheese melts and gently mix together.

Unroll the pastry and cover with waxed paper topped with a damp tea towel to prevent it from drying out, removing 1 sheet at a time. Brush 1 sheet of the pastry lightly with some of the 2 tablespoons melted butter. Top with another sheet of pastry and brush with melted butter. Spread $1/3$ of the crab meat mixture along the short end. Roll to enclose the filling, tucking the ends under. Brush with butter.

Arrange the roll seam side down on a baking sheet. Repeat the process with the remaining pastry, remaining butter and remaining crab meat mixture. Bake at 375 degrees for 20 to 25 minutes or until light brown. Cut each roll into 12 slices.

Makes 3 dozen

Swiss Tarts

4 puff pastry tart shells
9 slices bacon
1 medium onion, finely chopped
1 pound Swiss cheese, chopped or shredded
$3/4$ cup sour cream
2 eggs, lightly beaten
$1/8$ teaspoon salt
$1/8$ teaspoon pepper

Bake the pastry shells using package directions until golden brown. Let stand until cool. Remove the center cores and discard.

Fry the bacon in a skillet until crisp. Drain, reserving 2 tablespoons of the pan drippings. Crumble the bacon. Sauté the onion in the reserved pan drippings in the skillet until tender; drain. Combine the bacon, onion, Swiss cheese, sour cream, eggs, salt and pepper in a bowl and mix well.

Spoon the bacon mixture evenly into the tart shells. Arrange the shells on a baking sheet. Bake at 375 degrees for 12 to 15 minutes or until the cheese melts. Broil until light brown. Serve at your next luncheon or brunch with an avocado and grapefruit salad arranged on red leaf lettuce and drizzled with poppy seed dressing.

Serves 4

Photograph for this recipe is on page 172.

Crepes

Crepe is simply the French word for "pancake." Extremely versatile, crepes can be eaten as such, or with either a sweet or savory filling. The batter can be prepared with sugar for desserts, or with herbs for a savory presentation. Crepes can be prepared in advance and frozen sealed between sheets of waxed paper for up to two weeks. For basic crepes, sift 1 cup flour into a bowl. Whisk in 2/3 cup milk, 3 beaten eggs, 1 tablespoon beer and 1/4 teaspoon salt. Add 1/4 cup melted butter and whisk until smooth. Let stand for 45 minutes. Heat a 10-inch skillet over medium-high heat until hot. Brush with melted butter or spray with nonstick cooking spray. Ladle 1/4 cup of the batter into the skillet and swirl the skillet to spread the batter evenly over the bottom Cook for 30 seconds and flip. Cook for 15 seconds longer. Cool on a wire rack before storing. Repeat the process with the remaining batter.

Artichoke Bottoms with Spinach Stuffing

2 or 3 (14-ounce) cans whole artichoke bottoms, drained
Italian salad dressing
2 (10-ounce) packages frozen chopped spinach, thawed, drained
1/2 cup chopped onion
1/2 cup (1 stick) butter
1 cup sour cream
2 teaspoons red wine vinegar
1 teaspoon salt
1/8 teaspoon Worcestershire sauce
Freshly grated Parmesan cheese
Plain bread crumbs

Combine the artichoke bottoms with enough salad dressing to cover in a bowl. Marinate at room temperature while preparing the remaining ingredients.

Press the excess moisture from the spinach. Sauté the onion in the butter in a skillet until tender. Stir in the spinach, sour cream, wine vinegar, salt and Worcestershire sauce.

Drain the artichokes, discarding the marinade. Spoon some of the spinach mixture onto each artichoke bottom. Arrange the artichokes in a 3-quart baking dish. Sprinkle with cheese and bread crumbs. Bake at 350 degrees for 15 minutes. Serve immediately.

Serves 16

Lime Mousse

4 egg yolks or equivalent amount of egg substitute
1 cup sugar
$1/2$ cup fresh lime juice
Grated zest of 2 limes
1 envelope unflavored gelatin
$1/4$ cup cold water
1 cup whipping cream
4 to 5 egg whites
$1/8$ teaspoon salt
$1/2$ cup whipped cream
Lime zest and/or fresh mint leaves

Beat the egg yolks in a mixing bowl until pale yellow. Add the sugar, lime juice and zest of 2 limes. Beat until thickened.

Soften the gelatin in the cold water in a heatproof bowl. Place the bowl over hot water, stirring until the gelatin dissolves. Beat the gelatin into the egg yolk mixture. Place the egg yolk mixture in a pan of ice water to hasten the firming. Let stand until slightly congealed.

Beat 1 cup whipping cream in a mixing bowl until stiff peaks form. Beat the egg whites and salt in a mixing bowl until almost stiff. Fold the whipped cream into the egg yolk mixture and then fold in the egg whites. Spoon into a 1-quart soufflé dish. Chill for 1 hour or longer.

Spoon into dessert goblets. Top with $1/2$ cup whipped cream and additional lime zest and/or mint leaves. You may prepare up to 1 day in advance.

Serves 4 to 6

Mint Tea

Combine 2 family-size tea bags, 1 cup sugar, 3/4 cup packed mint leaves and juice of 3 lemons in a heatproof container. Pour 1 quart boiling water over the mixture. Steep, covered, for 5 to 10 minutes. Discard the tea bags and mint leaves. Pour the tea into a pitcher. Stir in 1 quart cold water. Pour over ice in glasses. Garnish with sprigs of fresh mint and lemon slices. Makes 2 quarts.

Frozen White Chocolate Terrine

4 cups heavy cream, chilled
1 cup melted white chocolate
1 cup melted dark chocolate
2 teaspoons vanilla extract
2 cups raspberry purée
Sprigs of fresh mint
Sifted confectioners' sugar
Shaved dark chocolate

Chill 2 mixing bowls. Line the bottom of a 5×9-inch loaf pan with parchment paper. Pour 2 cups of the heavy cream into each mixing bowl. Add 1 cup white chocolate to 1 bowl and 1 cup dark chocolate to the other bowl. Add 1 teaspoon of the vanilla to each bowl.

Beat the cream mixture in each mixing bowl for 3 to 4 minutes or until the mixtures are firm and velvety but still of a spreading consistency. Spread half the white chocolate mixture over the bottom of the prepared pan. Spread with half the dark chocolate mixture and top with the remaining white chocolate mixture, spreading evenly. Store the remaining chocolate mixture in the refrigerator. Freeze, covered with plastic wrap, for 2 hours or until set. Invert onto a serving platter.

Run the blade of a sharp knife under hot water. Cut the terrine into 2-inch slices using the heated knife. Spoon the remaining dark chocolate mixture into a pastry bag fitted with a star tip.

Spoon $1/3$ cup of the raspberry purée in the middle of each of 6 dessert plates. Top with 1 slice of the chocolate terrine. Pipe a small portion of the chocolate mixture off to the side of each slice. Top with sprigs of mint, confectioners' sugar and shaved chocolate.

Serves 6

Chocolate Raspberry Cake à la Simca

Raspberry Filling
$1^1/2$ pints fresh raspberries
$^1/3$ cup sugar
1 tablespoon crème de cassis

Cake
8 ounces semisweet chocolate
2 tablespoons instant espresso powder
$^1/4$ cup crème de cassis
4 egg yolks
$^3/4$ cup ($1^1/2$ sticks) unsalted butter
$^1/3$ cup bleached flour
4 egg whites
$^1/8$ teaspoon salt
$^1/3$ cup sugar

Chocolate Glaze
8 ounces semisweet chocolate
3 tablespoons crème de cassis
1 tablespoon water
1 tablespoon instant espresso powder

For the filling, toss the raspberries with the sugar and crème de cassis in a bowl.

For the cake, coat a 9-inch round cake pan with butter and dust lightly with flour. Line the bottom with waxed paper. Butter and flour the waxed paper, shaking to remove the excess. Combine the chocolate, espresso powder and crème de cassis in a heavy saucepan. Cook over low heat until the chocolate melts, stirring frequently. Remove from heat. Cool slightly. Add the egg yolks 1 at a time, mixing well after each addition. Return the saucepan to the heat. Cook for 2 minutes, stirring constantly. Remove from heat. Add the butter 1 tablespoon at a time, mixing after each addition until the butter melts. Stir in the flour. Beat the egg whites and salt in a mixing bowl until soft peaks form. Add the sugar gradually, beating constantly for 30 seconds or until glossy. Fold the egg whites $^1/3$ at a time into the chocolate mixture. Spoon the batter into the prepared pan. Bake at 375 degrees for 20 minutes or until the cake is slightly puffed but not completely cooked in the center. Cool in the pan on a wire rack for 45 minutes.

For the glaze, combine the chocolate, crème de cassis, water and espresso powder in a heavy saucepan. Cook over low heat until blended and of a glaze consistency, stirring frequently.

To assemble, invert the cake onto a cake plate; turn the cake right side up. Scoop out the top $^1/2$ inch of the cake, leaving a 1-inch border around the edge. Fill with the filling and pat lightly. Drizzle the cake with the warm glaze and spread to cover the top and side.

Serves 8 to 10

Austin
on the run

With a climate noted for its sunny days, Austin abounds with recreational offerings. More than 12,000 acres of undeveloped land, 175 parks, 23 green belts, and a veloway provide outdoor enthusiasts with a variety of venues to climb, row, bike, walk, skate, run, and enjoy just about any type of outdoor activity imaginable. Downtown Austin is bordered to the south by Town Lake, which is surrounded by more than 30 miles of trails, including the popular 10-mile Hike and Bike Trail. While walkers, joggers, and cyclists hug the trail along the tree-lined shore, canoeists and crews skim over the lake's surface.

Austin on the Run, Brunch on the Lawn

Beverages
    Screwdriver Twists
    Festive Bloody Marys
    Flaming Brandied Coffee

Appetizers
    Smoked Salmon Pouches
    Cream Cheese-Filled Strawberries

Entrées
    Eggs Benedict with Spinach and Smoked Salmon
    Cheesy Sausage Scramble
    Asparagus Chicken Quiche

Side Dishes
    Asparagus Caesar
    Savory Mushroom Cheesecake
    Tomato Tart
    Green Chile Cheese Grits

Breads
    Cheese Pennies
    Crunch Cake
    Peach Crumble Coffee Cake
    Crème Brûlée French Toast
    Macadamia Nut French Toast
    Lemon-Dipped Blueberry Muffins
        (pictured at right)

Screwdriver Twists

Combine 3¹/₂ *cups orange juice,* ¹/₂ *cup vodka, 2 teaspoons lemon juice and 2 teaspoons Triple Sec or other orange-flavor liqueur in a pitcher and mix well. Chill in the refrigerator. Pour over ice in glasses. Garnish with orange slices. Serves 4.*

Eggs Benedict with Spinach and Smoked Salmon

English Muffins
4 English muffins, split
Butter

Spinach
4 ounces fresh spinach, trimmed
2 tablespoons butter

Poached Eggs
1 tablespoon vinegar
8 eggs

Hollandaise Sauce and Assembly
3 egg yolks
2 tablespoons fresh lemon juice
¹/₂ cup (1 stick) butter, melted
¹/₈ teaspoon salt
¹/₈ teaspoon cayenne pepper
8 ounces smoked salmon

For the muffins, arrange the muffins cut side up on a baking sheet. Spread the cut sides with butter. Broil until light brown.

For the spinach, sauté the spinach in the butter in a skillet until spinach is wilted.

For the eggs, add just enough water to a saucepan to measure 2 inches. Bring to a simmer. Stir in the vinegar. Break the eggs 1 at a time gently into the water mixture; break the eggs as near the water as possible. Simmer for 3 minutes for a soft yolk or for up to 5 minutes for a firm yolk.

For the sauce, whisk the egg yolks and lemon juice in a double boiler until blended. Cook over hot water until slightly thickened, whisking constantly. Remove from heat. Add the melted butter to the egg yolk mixture gradually, whisking constantly until blended. Stir in the salt and cayenne pepper.

To assemble, place 1 muffin half toasted side up on each of 8 serving plates. Layer each muffin half with 1 tablespoon of the spinach, 1 poached egg, 1 ounce of the smoked salmon and 2 tablespoons of the hollandaise sauce. Serve immediately.

Serves 8

Cheesy Sausage Scramble

3/4 cup chopped onion
1/2 green bell pepper, chopped
4 to 6 tablespoons butter
8 to 12 ounces sausage
4 to 8 ounces mushrooms, chopped
1/4 cup sherry
1/8 teaspoon cumin
Salt and pepper to taste
Garlic powder to taste
12 eggs, beaten
1/2 cup shredded Cheddar cheese
4 1/2 drops of Tabasco sauce

Sauté the onion and bell pepper in the butter in a skillet until the onion is tender. Add the sausage. Cook until the sausage is brown and crumbly, stirring frequently. Stir in the mushrooms, sherry, cumin, salt, pepper and garlic powder.

Cook until the liquid is absorbed, stirring frequently. Combine the eggs, cheese, and Tabasco sauce in a bowl and mix well. Stir into the sausage mixture. Cook until the eggs are of the desired degree of doneness. Serve immediately with tortillas and roasted potatoes.

Serves 6

Festive Bloody Marys

Combine 4 1/2 *cups tomato juice, 3 tablespoons white wine Worcestershire sauce, 1/4 cup lime juice, 1 teaspoon celery salt, 1 teaspoon lemon pepper, 1/2 teaspoon coarsely ground pepper and 1/4 teaspoon hot sauce in a pitcher and mix well. Chill in the refrigerator. Stir in 1 cup vodka. Pour over ice in glasses. Garnish each serving with a rib of celery. Serves 6.*

Smoked Salmon Pouches

Cut 1 pound thinly sliced smoked salmon into halves. Combine 16 ounces softened cream cheese, 1/2 cup finely chopped red onion and 3 tablespoons chopped capers in a bowl and mix well. Spoon 1/2 teaspoon of the cream cheese mixture in the center of each half. Pinch and twist to enclose the filling and form a pouch. Chill, covered, until serving time. Makes approximately 40 pouches.

Asparagus Chicken Quiche

6 asparagus spears
1 recipe (1-crust) pie pastry (see page 213)
2 tablespoons snipped fresh chives or green onion tops
1 1/2 cups shredded Cheddar cheese
1 tablespoon flour
3 eggs, beaten
1/2 cup milk
1/8 teaspoon salt
1/8 teaspoon pepper
1/2 cup chopped cooked chicken or turkey
4 slices crisp-cooked bacon, crumbled

Break off the woody ends of the asparagus spears; the spears should be approximately 4 1/2 inches long. Cook the asparagus in boiling water in a saucepan for 5 minutes; drain.

Prepare the pastry, adding the chives or green onion tops with the flour and salt. Roll the dough into a 13-inch circle on a lightly floured surface. Fit the pastry into a 10-inch quiche dish; trim the edge. Line the bottom with a double thickness of heavy-duty foil. Bake at 450 degrees for 8 minutes; discard the foil. Bake for 4 to 5 minutes longer or until set and dry. Remove from oven. Reduce the oven temperature to 325 degrees.

Toss the cheese and flour in a bowl. Sprinkle over the hot pastry. Combine the eggs, milk, salt and pepper in a bowl and mix well. Stir in the chicken and bacon.

Pour over the cheese mixture. Arrange the asparagus in a spoke or fan pattern over the top. Bake at 325 degrees for 55 to 60 minutes or until a knife inserted near the center comes out clean. Let stand for 10 to 15 minutes before serving.

Serves 6

Asparagus Caesar

1 can anchovy fillets
2 pounds asparagus, trimmed, blanched
6 tablespoons freshly grated Parmesan cheese
3 tablespoons capers
2 tablespoons olive oil

Drain the anchovies, reserving the oil. Arrange the warm asparagus on a serving platter. Drizzle with the reserved anchovy oil. Sprinkle with the cheese and capers. Drizzle with the olive oil. Top with the anchovies.

Serves 4 to 6

Savory Mushroom Cheesecake

1 cup brown mushrooms, sliced
$1/2$ cup shiitake mushrooms, sliced
1 tablespoon butter
3 shallots, finely chopped
$1/2$ cup sun-dried tomatoes
1 head garlic, roasted
10 large fresh spinach leaves
16 ounces cream cheese, softened
3 eggs
Grated zest of 1 lemon
Salt and pepper to taste
Puréed roasted red peppers

Sauté the mushrooms in the butter in a skillet. Stir in the shallots, sun-dried tomatoes and garlic. Sauté briefly. Stir in the spinach. Sauté until the spinach wilts.

Beat the cream cheese in a mixing bowl until light and fluffy. Add the eggs and lemon zest. Beat until mixed. Season with salt and pepper. Stir in the mushroom mixture. Spoon the cream cheese mixture into a greased springform pan. Bake at 350 degrees until set. Serve with puréed roasted red peppers.

Serves 6 to 8

Tomato Tart

1 unbaked (9-inch) deep-dish pie shell
2 tablespoons Dijon mustard
8 ounces fresh mozzarella cheese, cut into $1/4$-inch slices
4 medium tomatoes, sliced
2 garlic cloves, minced
3 tablespoons chopped fresh basil
Salt and freshly ground pepper to taste
2 tablespoons extra-virgin olive oil

Bake the pie shell at 350 degrees for 10 minutes. Cool on a wire rack for 5 to 10 minutes. Spread the Dijon mustard over the bottom of the crust. Layer the cheese over the mustard. Arrange the tomato slices slightly overlapping in concentric circles over the cheese, beginning at the outer edge. Sprinkle with the garlic, basil, salt and pepper. Drizzle with the olive oil. Place the tart on a baking sheet. Bake at 350 degrees for 40 minutes or until golden brown. Cut into wedges.

Serves 4 to 6

Green Chile Cheese Grits

$3^{1}/_{2}$ cups water
1 cup quick-cooking white grits
4 ounces white Cheddar cheese, shredded
$1/3$ cup chopped green chiles
Salt and pepper to taste
Vegetable oil

Bring the water to a boil in a saucepan. Stir in the grits. Cook for 8 minutes, stirring frequently. Add the cheese, stirring until melted. Stir in the green chiles. Season with salt and pepper. Spoon the grits mixture into a greased 9×13-inch baking pan. Let stand until cool. Chill, covered, for 2 to 10 hours.

Cut the grits into 8 squares. Brush the squares with oil. Cook on a hot griddle or in a large nonstick skillet until light brown and crisp on both sides.

Serves 8

Cheese Pennies

8 ounces sharp Cheddar cheese, shredded, at room temperature
$1/2$ cup (1 stick) butter, softened
1 cup flour
$1/2$ envelope onion soup mix
$1/2$ teaspoon salt

Combine the cheese, butter, flour, soup mix and salt in a bowl and mix well. Shape the dough into 1-inch balls. Arrange 2 inches apart on a baking sheet. Flatten with a fork.

Bake at 400 degrees for 8 to 10 minutes or until light brown. Cool on the baking sheet for 2 minutes. Remove to a wire rack to cool completely. Store in an airtight container. This recipe may be doubled for a large crowd.

Makes 2 to 3 dozen

Crunch Cakes

Topping
$1^{1}/2$ cups vanilla wafer crumbs
1 cup chopped pecans
$1/3$ cup sugar

Filling
1 cup milk, at room temperature
1 cup (2 sticks) butter, softened
2 cups sugar
4 eggs, at room temperature
$1^{1}/2$ teaspoons vanilla extract
$2^{2}/3$ cups flour
$1^{1}/2$ teaspoons baking powder
$1/2$ teaspoon salt

For the topping, combine the vanilla wafer crumbs, pecans and sugar in a bowl and mix well. Pat the crumb mixture over the bottoms and up the sides of 2 greased 5×9-inch loaf pans.

For the filling, beat the milk, butter, sugar, eggs and vanilla in a mixing bowl until blended. Add a mixture of the flour, baking powder and salt. Beat until light and fluffy, scraping the bowl occasionally. Spoon the batter into the 2 prepared loaf pans.

Bake at 350 degrees for $1^{1}/2$ hours, covering with foil if needed to prevent overbrowning.

Serves 16

Peach Crumble Coffee Cake

Topping
1/2 cup sugar
1/3 cup flour
1 teaspoon cinnamon
1/4 cup (1/2 stick) butter, softened

Coffee Cake
2 cups flour
1 tablespoon baking powder
1/8 teaspoon salt
3/4 cup sugar
1/4 cup (1/2 stick) butter, softened
1 egg
1/2 cup milk
2 teaspoons vanilla extract
2 cups sliced fresh or frozen peaches

For the topping, combine the sugar, flour and cinnamon in a bowl and mix well. Add the butter and mix until crumbly.

For the coffee cake, sift the flour, baking powder and salt into a bowl and mix well. Beat the sugar and butter in a mixing bowl until creamy. Add the egg and beat until blended. Beat in the milk and vanilla until smooth. Add the flour mixture and mix well. Stir in the peaches. Spoon the batter into a greased and floured tube or bundt pan. Sprinkle with the topping.

Bake at 375 degrees for 45 minutes or until a wooden pick inserted near the center comes out clean. Invert onto a wire rack to cool. You may freeze for future use. As a variation, substitute your favorite fresh or frozen fruit for the peaches.

Serves 16

Crème Brûlée French Toast

1 cup packed brown sugar
$1/2$ cup (1 stick) unsalted butter
2 tablespoons corn syrup
8 (1-inch) slices French bread
$1^1/2$ cups half-and-half
5 eggs
1 teaspoon vanilla extract
1 teaspoon Grand Marnier
$1/4$ teaspoon salt

Heat the brown sugar, butter and corn syrup in a saucepan until blended, stirring frequently. Pour the brown sugar mixture into a 9×13-inch baking dish. Arrange the bread slices in a single layer over the prepared layer.

Whisk the half-and-half, eggs, vanilla, Grand Marnier and salt in a bowl until blended. Pour over the bread. Chill, covered, for 8 to 24 hours. Let stand until room temperature. Bake, uncovered, at 350 degrees for 35 to 40 minutes or until puffed and golden brown. Serve immediately.

Serves 8

Flaming Brandied Coffee

Rinse 1 heatproof beverage glass with hot water and pat dry. Pour 2 tablespoons of apricot brandy into the glass. Rotate the glass over a flame of an Irish coffee burner until the brandy ignites. Pour in 1 cup hot coffee and stir in 1 teaspoon sugar. Top with whipped cream. Sprinkle with nutmeg. Serves 1.

Cream Cheese-Filled Strawberries

Trim and core 16 large strawberries. Beat 8 ounces softened cream cheese, 2 tablespoons sugar and 1 tablespoon vanilla extract in a mixing bowl until light and fluffy, scraping the bowl occasionally. Spoon the cream cheese mixture into a pastry bag fitted with a star tip. Pipe into the strawberries. Garnish with almond slivers and fresh mint. Makes 16 filled strawberries.

Macadamia Nut French Toast

1 (1-pound) loaf Italian bread, cut into 1-inch slices
4 eggs, lightly beaten
$2/3$ cup orange juice
$2/3$ cup butter, melted
$1/3$ cup milk
$1/4$ cup sugar
1 teaspoon vanilla extract
$1/4$ teaspoon nutmeg
$1/2$ cup macadamia nuts, toasted, coarsely chopped

Arrange the bread slices in a single layer in a baking dish. Whisk the eggs, orange juice, butter, milk, sugar, vanilla and nutmeg in a bowl until blended. Pour over the bread. Soak, covered, in the refrigerator for 8 to 10 hours.

Arrange the bread slices on a greased baking sheet. Bake at 400 degrees for 10 minutes. Sprinkle with the macadamia nuts. Serve immediately with confectioners' sugar or syrup.

Serves 6 to 8

Lemon-Dipped Blueberry Muffins

Muffins

1 cup fresh blueberries
2 tablespoons sugar
2 teaspoons grated lemon zest
1^3/$_4$ cups flour
^{1}/$_2$ cup sugar
2^1/$_2$ teaspoons baking powder
^{3}/$_4$ teaspoon salt
^{3}/$_4$ cup milk
^{1}/$_3$ cup vegetable oil
1 egg, beaten

Topping

2 tablespoons butter, melted
^{1}/$_4$ teaspoon lemon juice
6 tablespoons sugar

For the muffins, toss the blueberries with 2 tablespoons sugar and lemon zest in a bowl. Combine the flour, ^{1}/$_2$ cup sugar, baking powder and salt in a bowl and mix well. Make a well in the center of the flour mixture.

Whisk the milk, oil and egg in a bowl until blended. Add to the well, stirring just until moistened. Fold in the blueberry mixture. Fill paper-lined or greased muffin cups ^{2}/$_3$ full. Bake at 400 degrees for 20 minutes or until golden brown.

For the topping, combine the butter and lemon juice in a bowl and mix well. Dip the warm muffins in the butter mixture and then in the sugar.

Makes 1 dozen muffins

Photograph for this recipe is on page 188.

Tea and Texas politics

The pink granite building finished in 1888 is the center of Texas state government. Its distinctive dome is crowned by the Goddess of Liberty. Since 1856, every Texas governor has called the gracious antebellum Governor's Mansion home. It serves as a museum of authentic period furnishings for visitors to admire. The Austin History Center specializes in current and historical materials about Austin and Travis County starting from the early 1800s. The landmark Texas State Cemetery is the final resting place of Texas' most notable sons and daughters, such as the Father of Texas Stephen F. Austin, writer J. Frank Dobie, former Governor John Connally, and stateswoman Barbara Jordan. One of the oldest monuments to Texas history is the six-hundred-year-old Treaty Oak, the sole survivor of a grove of oak trees where legend has it that Stephen F. Austin signed the first boundary treaty with the Tonkawa and Comanche Indians.

Menu

*Tea at the Governor's Mansion is a
Texas tradition. From baby showers to
bridal showers, use these menu choices
for your own special celebration!*

Beverages
Governor's Mansion Summer Peach Tea Punch
Coffee Ice Cream Punch

Appetizers
Sausage and Spinach in Phyllo
Tea-Smoked Shrimp Wrapped in Spinach
Curry Tea Sandwiches
Bitter Greens, Bleu Cheese and Chicken Sandwiches
Cucumber and Salmon Sandwiches
Favorite Chicken Salad
Asparagus au Citron

Desserts
Poppy Seed Strawberry Cake
Cream Cheese Bits
Grasshoppers
Hazelnut Raspberry Cookies
Lace Cookies
Scones
Lemon Curd Tartlets (pictured at right)

Governor's Mansion Summer Peach Tea Punch

Bring 6 cups water to a boil in a saucepan. Add 3 family-size tea bags and 2 cups loosely packed fresh mint. Let steep for 10 minutes; remove the tea bags. Cool to room temperature. Strain the tea into a 2-gallon container. Add one 32-ounce bottle R. W. Knudsen peach nectar, one 6-ounce can frozen lemonade concentrate and 1/2 to 1 cup simple syrup. Chill, covered, in the refrigerator. Pour into a punch bowl. Add one 1-liter bottle chilled ginger ale and one 1-liter bottle chilled club soda just before serving. To make a simple syrup, combine 2 cups sugar and 1 cup water in a saucepan. Bring to a boil. Boil for 4 minutes or until clear, stirring occasionally. Makes 40 (4-ounce) servings or about 1 1/4 gallons.

Sausage and Spinach in Phyllo

18 sheets frozen phyllo pastry
1 pound pork sausage
1/2 cup chopped onion
2 (10-ounce) packages frozen chopped spinach, cooked, drained
1 cup crumbled feta cheese
1/2 cup grated Parmesan cheese
1 teaspoon dried oregano, crushed
1/2 cup (1 stick) butter, melted

Thaw the pastry using package directions. Brown the sausage with the onion in a skillet, stirring until the sausage is crumbly; drain. Stir in the spinach, feta cheese, Parmesan cheese and oregano.

Unroll the pastry and cover with waxed paper topped with a damp tea towel to prevent it from drying out. Remove 1 sheet of the pastry and brush with some of the melted butter. Top with another sheet of the phyllo and brush with butter. Continue the process until you have 3 stacks, each containing 6 sheets. Spread 1/3 of the sausage mixture along 1 long edge of each pastry stack to within 2 inches of the short edges. Fold in the short edges. Roll to enclose the filling, beginning with the long edges spread with the sausage mixture.

Arrange the rolls on a baking sheet. Brush with the remaining butter. Score crosswise at 1-inch intervals with a sharp knife, cutting just to the filling. Bake at 350 degrees for 25 to 30 minutes or until brown. Slice where scored.

Makes 3 dozen

Tea-Smoked Shrimp Wrapped in Spinach

Shrimp
1/2 cup flour
1/2 cup packed brown sugar
1/2 cup Lapsang Souchong tea leaves
2 pounds large shrimp (about 60), peeled, deveined
1/2 cup sesame oil

Wrapping and Assembly
8 ounces fresh spinach leaves
2 bunches chives

For the shrimp, line a wok with foil, allowing enough overhang to form a tent over the shrimp. Combine the flour, brown sugar and tea leaves in the wok. Place a rack over the mixture. Arrange the shrimp on the rack and tent the foil to cover the shrimp; cover with a lid.

Cook over high heat until the ingredients begin to smoke. Cook for 5 minutes longer. Turn off the heat. Let stand, covered, for 10 minutes. Remove the cover gradually and gently unseal the foil. Remove the shrimp and brush lightly with the sesame oil.

For the wrapping, blanch the spinach in boiling water in a saucepan for 30 seconds. Drain and rinse with cold water. Spread the spinach leaves on a tea towel to drain. Blanch the chives in boiling water in a saucepan; drain. Rinse with cold water and pat dry. Cut the spines from the spinach leaves and cut each leaf into 1-inch strips.

To assemble, wrap a spinach strip around the middle of each shrimp, allowing the pink ends of the shrimp to show. Wrap and tie each with a chive. Serve with soy sauce for dipping.

Serves 10

Curry Tea Sandwiches

Beat 8 ounces softened cream cheese, 1/4 cup orange marmalade and 1 1/2 teaspoons curry powder in a mixing bowl until blended. Stir in 1/3 cup chopped toasted almonds. Spread on thinly sliced white bread. Makes 2 dozen sandwiches.

Bitter Greens, Bleu Cheese and Chicken Sandwiches

2 ounces bleu cheese, crumbled
3 tablespoons butter, softened
2 tablespoons sour cream
6 large slices sourdough bread
12 endive leaves
12 chicory leaves
1/3 cup olive oil
1 tablespoon lemon juice
1 teaspoon sugar
1 teaspoon whole grain mustard
8 ounces cooked chicken, thinly sliced
2 ounces bleu cheese, crumbled
1 small pear, thinly sliced
1/2 cup pecans, toasted
Freshly ground pepper to taste

Combine 2 ounces bleu cheese, butter and sour cream in a food processor. Process until smooth. Spread the mixture over 1 side of each of the bread slices.

Toss the endive and chicory in a bowl. Whisk the olive oil, lemon juice, sugar and mustard in a bowl. Drizzle over the endive mixture and toss to coat. Layer the bread slices with the endive mixture, chicken, 2 ounces bleu cheese, sliced pear and pecans in the order listed. Sprinkle with pepper and serve open-faced.

Makes 6 sandwiches

Cucumber and Salmon Sandwiches

6 ounces cream cheese, softened
4 ounces smoked salmon
$1/4$ cup finely chopped cucumber
1 teaspoon minced watercress
$1/2$ teaspoon lemon juice
Salt and pepper to taste
12 slices extra-thin sandwich bread, crusts removed
3 tablespoons butter, softened
$1/2$ cup minced watercress

Combine the cream cheese, salmon, cucumber, 1 teaspoon watercress, lemon juice, salt and pepper in a food processor container. Process until blended.

Spread the cream cheese mixture over 1 side of half the bread slices. Top with the remaining bread slices. Cut the sandwiches into desired shapes. Spread the outer edges of the sandwiches with the butter. Coat the buttered edges with $1/2$ cup minced watercress.

Makes 6 sandwiches

Tea sandwiches are traditionally dainty sandwiches served on thinly sliced bread, sometimes open-faced, and always presented in a most appealing way. They should be as beautiful to behold as they are delicious to eat. Tea sandwiches tend to be lighter-than-usual mealtime sandwiches, but from there the possibilities have few limits. We've already given you some delicious options, but don't stop with our ideas. Some of our other favorite combinations include: smoked salmon on pumpernickel with sprigs of fresh dillweed; dates with cream cheese on wheat; sliced hard-cooked eggs on wheat bread spread with lemon mayonnaise and sprinkled with caviar; ham with asparagus on herb-buttered wheat bread; thinly sliced turkey with raspberry jam on rye bread with mustard and watercress; and prosciutto with cream cheese on rye.

Favorite Chicken Salad

4 large boneless skinless chicken breasts, poached, chopped
$1/2$ cup chopped celery
$1/2$ cup chopped green apple
$1/4$ cup golden raisins
$1/4$ cup dark raisins
1 teaspoon tarragon
1 cup mayonnaise
$1/4$ to $1/3$ cup orange juice

Combine the chicken, celery, green apple, golden raisins, dark raisins and tarragon in a bowl and mix well. Stir in a mixture of the mayonnaise and orange juice. Chill, covered, until serving time.

Spoon the chicken salad into lettuce cups or over field greens on serving plates. Or use as a spread on your favorite bread. Garnish with sliced fresh fruit or edible flowers.

Serves 6 to 8

Asparagus au Citron

$1^1/2$ pounds fresh asparagus spears
$1/4$ cup fresh lemon juice
$1/4$ cup dry white wine
3 tablespoons extra-virgin olive oil
2 tablespoons sugar
1 tablespoon grated lemon zest

Blanch the asparagus in boiling water in a saucepan for 2 to 3 minutes or until al dente; drain.

Whisk the lemon juice, wine, olive oil, sugar and lemon zest in a bowl until mixed. Arrange the asparagus on a serving platter. Drizzle with the lemon juice mixture. Garnish with additional lemon zest.

Serves 4

Poppy Seed Strawberry Cake

Cake

3 cups cake flour
2 teaspoons baking powder
$1/2$ teaspoon baking soda
$1/2$ teaspoon salt
2 cups sugar
1 cup (2 sticks) butter, softened
1 tablespoon plus 1 teaspoon grated lemon zest
4 eggs
2 tablespoons lemon juice
$1^1/2$ teaspoons vanilla extract
1 cup buttermilk
2 tablespoons poppy seeds

White Chocolate Frosting and Topping

$3/4$ cup sugar
2 eggs
6 tablespoons lemon juice
$1^1/3$ cups (8 ounces) white chocolate chips
3 cups whipping cream
$1/4$ cup sugar
2 cups sliced fresh strawberries

For the cake, combine the cake flour, baking powder, baking soda and salt in a bowl and mix well. Beat the sugar, butter and lemon zest in a mixing bowl until creamy. Add the eggs 1 at a time, beating well after each addition. Beat in the lemon juice and vanilla. Add the dry ingredients in 3 batches alternately with the buttermilk, mixing well after each addition. Stir in the poppy seeds. Spoon the batter into 3 greased 9-inch cake pans. Bake at 350 degrees for 25 minutes. Cool in the pans for 10 minutes. Remove to a wire rack to cool completely.

For the frosting, whisk $3/4$ cup sugar, eggs and lemon juice in a double boiler over simmering water. Simmer for 3 minutes or until thickened, whisking constantly. Remove from the heat. Add the white chocolate chips, stirring until blended. Cool to room temperature.

Beat the whipping cream and $1/4$ cup sugar in a mixing bowl until soft peaks form. Fold into the white chocolate mixture.

To assemble, place 1 cake layer on a cake plate. Spread with 1 cup of the frosting. Top with 1 cup of the strawberries and $1/2$ cup of the frosting. Top with another cake layer. Spread with 1 cup of the frosting, remaining 1 cup strawberries and $1/2$ cup of the frosting. Top with the remaining cake layer. Spread with the remaining frosting.

Serves 12

Cream Cheese Bits

Graham cracker crumbs
16 ounces cream cheese, softened
$3/4$ cup sugar
3 each egg yolks and egg whites
1 cup sour cream
$3/4$ cup sugar
$1/2$ teaspoon vanilla extract

Sprinkle graham cracker crumbs over the bottoms and up the sides of greased miniature muffin cups. Beat the cream cheese, $3/4$ cup sugar and egg yolks in a mixing bowl until creamy. Beat the egg whites in a mixing bowl until stiff peaks form. Fold the egg whites into the creamed mixture. Fill the prepared muffin cups $3/4$ full. Bake at 350 degrees for 20 minutes. Cool in the pans for 10 minutes. Remove to a wire rack to cool completely. Beat the sour cream, $3/4$ cup sugar and vanilla in a mixing bowl until blended. Spoon into a 9-inch-round baking dish. Bake at 400 degrees for 5 minutes; stir. Bake for 3 minutes. Spoon 1 tablespoon sour cream mixture over the top of each cheese bit. Chill before serving.

Makes 3 dozen

Grasshoppers

$1^1/4$ cups ($2^1/2$ sticks) butter
$1/2$ cup baking cocoa
$3^1/2$ cups confectioners' sugar
1 egg, lightly beaten
1 teaspoon vanilla extract
2 cups graham cracker crumbs
$1/3$ cup crème de menthe
$1^1/2$ cups (9 ounces) semisweet chocolate chips

Combine $1/2$ cup of the butter and baking cocoa in a saucepan. Cook until blended, stirring frequently. Remove from heat. Stir in $1/2$ cup of the confectioners' sugar, egg and vanilla. Stir in the graham cracker crumbs. Press the crumb mixture over the bottom of an ungreased 9×13-inch baking pan. Heat $1/2$ cup of the butter in a saucepan until melted. Stir in the crème de menthe. Remove from heat. Beat in the remaining 3 cups confectioners' sugar until blended. Spread over the crumb layer. Chill for 1 hour. Combine the remaining $1/4$ cup butter and chocolate chips in a saucepan. Cook over low heat until blended, stirring frequently. Spread over the prepared layers. Chill for 1 to 2 hours or until set. Let stand at room temperature for 15 minutes before cutting into squares.

Makes 4 dozen squares

Hazelnut Raspberry Cookies

1 cup hazelnuts, toasted
$2/3$ cup sugar
3 cups flour
$1/4$ teaspoon salt
$1/4$ teaspoon baking powder
$1^1/4$ cups ($2^1/2$ sticks) unsalted butter, softened
1 egg
1 egg yolk
1 teaspoon vanilla extract
$1^1/4$ cups raspberry jam
Confectioners' sugar

Process the hazelnuts and sugar in a food processor until ground. Combine the flour, salt and baking powder in a bowl and mix well. Beat the butter in a mixing bowl until light and fluffy, scraping the bowl occasionally. Add the hazelnut mixture. Beat until mixed. Beat in the egg, egg yolk and vanilla. Add the dry ingredients and mix well. Divide the dough into 4 equal portions. Flatten each portion into a disk. Wrap each disk in plastic wrap. Chill for 2 hours or until firm.

Remove 1 dough disk from the refrigerator. Roll the disk $1/8$ inch thick on a lightly floured surface. Cut the dough with a 3-inch cookie cutter. Arrange the cookies $1/2$ inch apart on an ungreased cookie sheet. Reshape the leftover dough into a disk. Chill, wrapped in plastic wrap, in the refrigerator. Bake the cookies at 325 degrees for 10 minutes or until golden brown. Repeat the process with the remaining dough and leftover dough.

Bring the jam to a boil in a saucepan. Boil for 4 minutes or until thickened, stirring constantly. Spread 1 teaspoon of the jam to within $1/4$ inch of the edges of half the cookies. Sift confectioners' sugar lightly over the remaining cookies. Top the cookies spread with jam with the cookies sprinkled with confectioners' sugar to make a sandwich. You may prepare these cookies up to 2 weeks in advance and store in a single layer in an airtight container in the refrigerator.

Makes 4 dozen cookies

Coffee Ice Cream Punch

Combine 1 gallon cool strong coffee, 1 quart milk and 1 cup sugar in a large container and mix well. Chill, covered, for 24 hours. Just before serving, spoon 1/2 gallon chocolate ice cream into a punch bowl. Pour the coffee mixture over the ice cream. Beat 2 cups whipping cream in a mixing bowl until soft peaks form. Add 3 tablespoons sugar and 1 tablespoon vanilla extract. Beat until blended. Float the whipped cream on top of the punch. Sprinkle with grated semisweet chocolate. Serves 20.

Scones

2 cups flour, sifted
3 tablespoons sugar
1 tablespoon baking powder
1/2 teaspoon salt
1/2 cup (1 stick) butter, softened
2/3 cup light or heavy cream
1 egg
Currants to taste
Chopped walnuts to taste
Melted butter
Sugar or cinnamon-sugar

Sift the flour, sugar, baking powder and salt into a bowl and mix well. Cut in the butter until crumbly. Stir in a mixture of the light cream and egg. Add the currants and walnuts and mix well. The dough will be very sticky.

Knead the dough on a lightly floured surface, adding additional flour as needed to make an easily handled dough. Cut or shape the dough as desired. Arrange on a baking sheet. Brush the tops with melted butter and sprinkle with additional sugar or cinnamon-sugar mixture. Bake at 425 degrees for 15 minutes. You may prepare in advance and freeze unbaked. Thaw before baking.

Makes 20 scones

Lemon Curd Tartlets

Pastry

2 1/2 cups flour
1 teaspoon salt
1 teaspoon sugar
1 cup (2 sticks) unsalted butter, chopped
1/4 to 1/2 cup ice water

Lemon Filling

2 cups sugar
12 egg yolks, lightly beaten
1 cup lemon juice
1 cup (2 sticks) unsalted butter
2 tablespoons grated lemon zest

For the pastry, combine the flour, salt and sugar in a food processor. Add the butter gradually, processing constantly for 10 seconds or until crumbly. Add the ice water 1/2 teaspoon at a time, processing constantly until the dough forms a ball. Chill, covered with plastic wrap, for 1 hour.

Roll the dough 1/8 inch thick between sheets of waxed paper. Cut the dough to fit twelve 2- to 3-inch tartlet cups. Fit the dough over the bottoms and up the sides of the cups. The pastry recipe makes enough pastry for two 8- to 10-inch tart or pie shells or one 2-crust pie.

For the filling, whisk the sugar and egg yolks in a saucepan. Stir in the lemon juice. Cook over low heat until a candy thermometer registers 168 degrees or the mixture coats the back of a wooden spoon, stirring constantly; do not boil. Remove from heat. Whisk until slightly cooled. Whisk in the butter and lemon zest. Let stand until cool. Spoon into the tartlet shells. Garnish with lemon zest, crystallized violets or fresh raspberries.

Makes 1 dozen tartlets

Photograph for this recipe is on page 202.

Lace Cookies

Combine 1 cup finely ground almonds, 3/4 cup sugar, 1/2 cup (1 stick) melted butter, 2 tablespoons milk and 4 teaspoons flour in a mixing bowl. Beat until smooth. Shape the dough by tablespoonfuls into 3-inch circles. Arrange 3 to 4 inches apart on a parchment-lined cookie sheet. Bake at 350 degrees for 10 to 12 minutes or until brown. The cookies will be approximately 5 inches in diameter. Makes 3 dozen cookies.

Kid *Friendly*

Children are special citizens in the Capital City. Zilker Park offers swimming in Barton Springs, where the temperature remains sixty-eight degrees year-round; hike-and-bike trails; playgrounds; picnic facilities; canoe rentals; and a miniature train to tour Austin's most popular park. Always a hit with the younger set, the Austin Children's Museum offers educational and entertaining hands-on exhibits and programs. The Austin Nature and Science Center is a living science museum that includes a discovery lab, exhibits on the nature of Austin, live animals, and an Eco-Detective Trail. If a full-size train is more appealing, take a relaxing scenic journey aboard the Hill Country Flyer, Central Texas' vintage steam train. Some of the most unique visitors to Austin are the 1.5 million Mexican free-tail bats that make their summer home under Austin's Congress Avenue bridge. Their nightly exodus each summer brings a look of awe to all children, young and old, as the thousands of small creatures create a ribbon of black unfurling across the evening sky.

The Junior League of Austin celebrates children!

Beverages
Front Porch Lemonade
Old-Fashioned Hot Chocolate

Entrées
Spaghetti Bake
Spaghetti Sauce with Meatballs
Parmesan Chicken Strips
Macaroni and Cheese

Side Dishes
Candied Carrots
Barbecued Corn

Breads
Cinnamon Twists
Grilled Strawberry Bread
Pumpkin Chip Muffins

Desserts
Dirt Cake
Gingersnaps
Peppermint Candy Canes
Thumbprint Jelly Cookies
   (pictured at right)
Tiger Butter
Sugar Cookies
Snickerdoodles
Peanut Brittle Crispies
Buttermilk Cake
Versatile Cream Cheese Frosting
Rich Brownie Cupcakes

Front Porch Lemonade

Dissolve 1³/4 cups sugar in 1 cup boiling water in a heatproof container. Stir in 4¹/2 cups cold water and 1¹/2 cups fresh lemon juice. Chill. Pour over ice in glasses. Garnish with lemon slices. Serves 8.

Spaghetti Bake

8 ounces spaghetti
4 slices bacon
¹/2 cup finely chopped onion
2 cups cream
2 eggs
1 cup green peas
1 cup grated Parmesan cheese

Cook the pasta using package directions; drain. Spoon into a 9×13-inch baking dish sprayed with nonstick cooking spray.

Cook the bacon in a skillet until crisp. Drain, reserving the bacon drippings. Crumble the bacon. Sauté the onion in the reserved bacon drippings until tender; drain.

Whisk the cream and eggs in a saucepan until blended. Stir in the bacon, onion and peas. Simmer for 10 minutes, stirring frequently; do not boil. Spoon over the pasta. Sprinkle with the cheese. Bake at 350 degrees for 20 to 30 minutes or until bubbly.

Serves 4 to 6

Spaghetti Sauce with Meatballs

Spaghetti Sauce
3/4 cup chopped onion
1 garlic clove, chopped
3 tablespoons vegetable oil
2 (16-ounce) cans Italian tomatoes
2 (6-ounce) cans tomato paste
1 cup water
1 tablespoon sugar
1 1/2 teaspoons salt
1 1/2 teaspoons dried oregano
1/2 teaspoon pepper
1 bay leaf

Meatballs
1/2 cup milk
2 eggs
1/4 cup bread crumbs
1 pound ground beef
1/4 pound ground pork
1/2 cup grated Parmesan cheese
1/2 cup chopped onion
1 garlic clove, minced
1 tablespoon Italian seasoning
1/2 teaspoon salt
Pepper to taste
3 tablespoons olive oil

For the sauce, sauté the onion and garlic in the oil in a large saucepan until tender. Stir in the undrained tomatoes, tomato paste, water, sugar, salt, oregano, pepper and bay leaf. Simmer, covered, for 1 hour, stirring occasionally.

For the meatballs, whisk the milk and eggs in a large bowl until blended. Soak the bread crumbs in the milk mixture until softened. Add the ground beef, ground pork, cheese, onion, garlic, Italian seasoning, salt and pepper and mix well. Shape into 1-inch balls.

Sauté the meatballs in the olive oil in a skillet until brown and cooked through; drain. Add to the sauce and mix gently. Simmer, covered, for 1 hour, stirring occasionally. Discard the bay leaf. Spoon the sauce and meatballs over spaghetti or your favorite pasta on a serving platter.

Serves 6 to 8

Parmesan Chicken Strips

4 boneless skinless chicken breasts
1/2 cup grated Parmesan cheese
1/2 cup bread crumbs
1 tablespoon dried Italian seasoning
Salt and pepper to taste
2 eggs, lightly beaten
1/2 cup flour
3 to 4 tablespoons olive oil

Pound the chicken 1/2 inch thick between sheets of waxed paper. Cut each chicken breast lengthwise into 2 or 3 strips. Combine the cheese, bread crumbs, Italian seasoning, salt and pepper in a shallow dish.

Dip the chicken strips in the eggs and then coat with the flour. Dip the chicken in the eggs again and then in the cheese mixture. Sauté the chicken in the olive oil in a skillet over medium heat for 3 minutes per side or until brown and cooked through. Serve with spaghetti sauce.

Serves 3 or 4

Macaroni and Cheese

16 ounces elbow macaroni
1/3 cup butter
1/3 cup flour
3 cups milk
2 teaspoons salt
1 teaspoon pepper
3 to 4 cups shredded Cheddar cheese

Cook the pasta using package directions until al dente; drain. Cover to keep warm. Heat the butter in a saucepan until melted. Stir in the flour. Cook over medium heat until light brown, stirring constantly. Reduce the heat to low. Whisk in the milk, salt and pepper. Cook until thickened, whisking constantly. Remove from heat. Add 2 to 3 cups of the cheese and stir until blended.

Add the pasta to the cheese mixture and mix well. Spoon the pasta mixture into a greased baking dish. Sprinkle with the remaining 1 to 2 cups cheese. Bake at 350 degrees for 20 minutes or until light brown.

Serves 6 to 8

Candied Carrots

16 ounces carrots
$^1/_2$ cup (1 stick) butter
1 cup sugar
Almond extract to taste

Peel the carrots and julienne or coarsely grate. Place the carrots in a large heavy saucepan. Top with the butter. Sprinkle with the sugar and drizzle with almond extract. Add just enough water to cover the carrots.

Cook, covered, over medium heat until the butter melts; remove the cover. Simmer for 2 hours or until the carrots are candied. Do not substitute margarine for the butter in this recipe. You may prepare the carrots up to 1 week in advance and store, covered, in the refrigerator. Heat for 15 minutes before serving.

Serves 6

Barbecued Corn

6 ears of unhusked corn
Melted butter
Seasoned salt to taste
Lime juice to taste

Pull the corn husks back carefully, leaving the husks attached at the base of the cob and removing the silk. Soak the corn in enough water to cover in a large bowl for 20 to 30 minutes. Drain and pat dry.

Brush the corn kernels with a mixture of butter, seasoned salt and lime juice. Reposition the husks and secure with kitchen twine. Grill over hot coals for 15 minutes. Discard the kitchen twine and pull the husks back. Tie the husks at the base to form a handle. Vary the seasonings according to taste.

Serves 6

Cinnamon Twists

Filling
$1/4$ cup ($1/2$ stick) butter, softened
$1/4$ cup packed brown sugar
1 teaspoon cinnamon
$1/2$ teaspoon vanilla extract

Pastry
$3^3/4$ cups flour
1 cup hot water
6 tablespoons butter, softened
$1/3$ cup sugar
$1/4$ cup nonfat dry milk powder
1 egg, lightly beaten
1 tablespoon fast-rising yeast
1 teaspoon salt
1 teaspoon nutmeg
1 teaspoon cinnamon
1 teaspoon vanilla extract
Melted butter

Cinnamon Topping
$1/4$ cup ($1/2$ stick) butter, melted
$1/2$ cup sugar
$1^1/2$ teaspoons cinnamon

For the filling, beat the butter, brown sugar, cinnamon and vanilla in a mixing bowl until creamy.

For the pastry, combine the flour, hot water, 6 tablespoons butter, sugar, milk powder, egg, yeast, salt, nutmeg, cinnamon and vanilla in a bowl and mix well. Knead for 6 to 8 minutes or until smooth and elastic. Let rise, covered, for 1 to $1^1/2$ hours or until doubled in bulk.

Roll the pastry into a 12×20-inch rectangle on a lightly floured surface. Spread the filling evenly over half the pastry. Fold the dough over the filling and roll gently to seal. Cut into fifteen $3/4$-inch strips, each about 12 inches long. Twist the strips gently and arrange on a lightly greased baking sheet. Let rise for 30 to 45 minutes. Spritz the twists lightly with water. Bake at 375 degrees for 12 to 14 minutes or until light brown. Brush with melted butter.

For the topping, combine the butter, sugar and cinnamon in a bowl and mix well. Sprinkle over the hot twists.

Makes 15 twists

Grilled Strawberry Bread

6 slices bread
$^1/_4$ cup ($^1/_2$ stick) butter
2 cups sliced fresh strawberries
6 to 12 tablespoons sugar

Sauté the bread in the butter in a skillet until brown on both sides. Spoon $^1/_3$ cup of the strawberries onto each bread slice. Sprinkle with the sugar and press lightly. Serve immediately.

Serves 6

Pumpkin Chip Muffins

3 cups flour
2 teaspoons baking soda
2 teaspoons baking powder
1 teaspoon cinnamon
1 teaspoon salt
1 (16-ounce) can pumpkin
2 cups sugar
$1^1/_2$ cups vegetable oil
4 eggs
2 cups (12 ounces) chocolate chips

Combine the flour, baking soda, baking powder, cinnamon and salt in a bowl and mix well. Beat the pumpkin, sugar, oil and eggs in a mixing bowl until smooth. Add the flour mixture and mix just until moistened. Fold in the chocolate chips. Fill greased or paper-lined muffin cups $^3/_4$ full. Bake at 400 degrees for 16 to 20 minutes or until the muffins test done. Cool in the pan for 10 minutes. Remove to a wire rack to cool completely.

Makes 2 dozen muffins

Old-Fashioned Hot Chocolate

Combine 4 ounces unsweetened chocolate and 1 cup water in a saucepan. Cook for 4 minutes or until the chocolate melts, stirring frequently. Stir in 1 cup sugar and $^1/_4$ teaspoon salt. Cook for 30 seconds and stir. Remove from heat. Stir in $^1/_2$ teaspoon vanilla extract. For each serving, spoon 2 to 3 tablespoons of the chocolate syrup into a microwave-safe mug. Fill $^2/_3$ full with milk and stir. Microwave for $1^3/_4$ minutes. Top with miniature marshmallows. Serve immediately.

Dirt Cake

8 ounces cream cheese, softened
1 cup confectioners' sugar
$1/4$ cup ($1/2$ stick) margarine
$3^1/4$ cups milk
12 ounces whipped topping
2 (4-ounce) packages vanilla instant pudding mix
1 (20-ounce) package chocolate sandwich cookies, crushed

Beat the cream cheese, confectioners' sugar and margarine in a mixing bowl until smooth. Whisk the milk, whipped topping and pudding mix in a bowl until blended. Add to the cream cheese mixture and mix well.

Line a sterile new flowerpot with plastic wrap. Spread $1/3$ of the crushed cookies over the bottom. Layer with half the pudding mixture and half the remaining cookies. Top with the remaining pudding mixture and remaining cookies. Insert a flower in the center. Chill until serving time.

Serves 8

Gingersnaps

2 cups flour
2 teaspoons baking soda
$1/2$ teaspoon ground cloves
$1/2$ teaspoon ginger
$1/4$ teaspoon salt
1 cup sugar
$3/4$ cup shortening
1 egg
$1/4$ cup molasses
Sugar to taste

Sift the flour, baking soda, cloves, ginger and salt into a bowl and mix well. Beat 1 cup sugar and shortening in a mixing bowl until creamy. Add the egg and beat until blended. Beat in the molasses. Add the flour mixture and mix well. Chill, covered, for 1 hour.

Shape the dough into 1-inch balls. Roll in sugar to taste. Arrange the cookies 2 inches apart on a cookie sheet. Bake at 375 degrees for 8 to 10 minutes or until crisp around the edges. Cool on the cookie sheet for 2 minutes. Remove to a wire rack to cool completely.

Makes 2 dozen cookies

Peppermint Candy Canes

1 cup shortening
1 cup confectioners' sugar
1 egg
$1^1/_2$ teaspoons almond extract
1 teaspoon vanilla extract
$2^1/_2$ cups flour
1 teaspoon salt
$^1/_2$ teaspoon red food coloring
$^1/_2$ cup crushed peppermint candy canes
$^1/_2$ cup sugar

Beat the shortening, confectioners' sugar, egg and flavorings in a mixing bowl until smooth. Add a mixture of the flour and salt and mix well. Divide the dough into 2 equal portions. Add the red food coloring to 1 portion and mix well. Roll 1 teaspoon of each dough portion into a log and twist together. Shape into a candy cane on a cookie sheet. Repeat the process with the remaining dough. Bake at 375 degrees for 9 minutes. Sprinkle with a mixture of the crushed candy and sugar. Cool on the cookie sheet for 2 minutes. Remove to a wire rack to cool completely.

Makes 2 to 3 dozen cookies

Thumbprint Jelly Cookies

1 cup (2 sticks) butter, softened
$^1/_2$ cup sugar
2 cups flour
Egg whites, lightly beaten
Ground pecans (optional)
Jam or jelly

Beat the butter in a mixing bowl until creamy. Add the sugar and beat until light and fluffy. Beat in the flour. Shape the dough into $^3/_4$-inch balls. Dip the balls in egg whites and roll in pecans. Arrange on a cookie sheet. Bake at 350 degrees for 5 minutes.

Make an indentation in the center of each hot cookie with the thumb or the back of a spoon. Fill the indentations with jam or jelly. Bake for 15 minutes longer or until light brown. Cool on the cookie sheet for 2 minutes. Remove to a wire rack to cool completely. As an alternative to jam or jelly, the indentations may be filled with frosting after the cookies have been baked and decorated with sprinkles or marshmallows.

Makes 2 dozen cookies

Photograph for this recipe is on page 216.

Tiger Butter

Combine 1 pound vanilla almond bark and 1/2 cup crunchy peanut butter in a saucepan. Cook over low heat until melted, stirring frequently. Spread in a thin layer on a foil-lined baking sheet. Microwave 1/2 cup chocolate chips in a microwave-safe dish until melted. Drizzle over the peanut butter layer and swirl. Let stand until firm. Break into bite-size pieces.

Sugar Cookies

4 cups flour
1 teaspoon baking soda
1 teaspoon salt
1 teaspoon cream of tartar
1 cup butter, softened
1 cup confectioners' sugar
1 cup sugar
1 cup vegetable oil
2 eggs
1 teaspoon vanilla extract
1 cup sugar

Sift the flour, baking soda, salt and cream of tartar into a bowl and mix well. Beat the butter, confectioners' sugar and 1 cup sugar in a mixing bowl until creamy. Add the oil and beat until smooth. Beat in the eggs and vanilla. Add the flour mixture and mix well. Chill, covered, until firm.

Shape the dough into 1-inch balls. Roll in 1 cup sugar. Arrange on a cookie sheet. Press each ball gently with a fork to flatten. Bake at 375 degrees for 10 minutes or until light brown. Cool on the cookie sheet for 2 minutes. Remove to a wire rack to cool completely.

For future use, freeze the dough balls on cookie sheets. Remove to sealable plastic freezer bags for storage. Freeze until just before baking.

Makes 7 dozen cookies

Snickerdoodles

Melted butter
2 cups flour
$1/2$ teaspoon baking soda
$1/4$ teaspoon salt
$1/8$ teaspoon (heaping) freshly grated nutmeg
$3/4$ cup sugar
$1/2$ cup unsalted butter, softened
1 egg
1 egg yolk
1 teaspoon vanilla extract
1 teaspoon finely grated lemon or orange zest
2 tablespoons sugar
2 teaspoons cinnamon

Brush 2 cookie sheets with melted butter. Sift the flour, baking soda, salt and nutmeg into a bowl and mix well. Beat $3/4$ cup sugar and $1/2$ cup butter in a mixing bowl until creamy. Add the egg, egg yolk, vanilla and lemon zest. Beat until light and fluffy, scraping the bowl occasionally. Add the flour mixture and mix well. Chill, covered with plastic wrap, for 30 minutes.

Combine 2 tablespoons sugar and cinnamon in a bowl and mix well. Shape just enough of the dough by teaspoonfuls into 1-inch balls to fill the prepared cookie sheets, leaving the remaining dough in the refrigerator. Roll the balls in the cinnamon and sugar mixture. Arrange 2 inches apart on the prepared cookie sheets. Flatten slightly with a glass.

Bake at 375 degrees for 12 minutes or just until the cookies begin to brown around the edges. Cool on the cookie sheets for 2 minutes. Remove to a wire rack to cool completely. Repeat the process with the remaining dough and remaining cinnamon and sugar mixture, preparing the cookie sheets as directed before baking each batch of cookies.

Makes 3 dozen cookies

Peanut Brittle Crispies

Beat one 1-pound package confectioners' sugar, 2 cups peanut butter and $3/4$ cup ($1^1/2$ sticks) melted margarine in a mixing bowl until blended. Stir in $4^1/2$ cups crisp rice cereal. Spread the cereal mixture in a greased 9×13-inch pan. Heat 6 squares chocolate bark in a double boiler over simmering water until melted. Spread over the top. Chill until set. Cut into squares. Makes 3 dozen squares.

Buttermilk Cake

2 cups flour
$^1/_2$ teaspoon baking soda
$^1/_2$ teaspoon baking powder
$^1/_8$ teaspoon salt
2 cups sugar
1 cup (2 sticks) butter, softened
4 eggs
1 cup buttermilk
1 teaspoon vanilla extract
1 cup heavy cream
$2^1/_2$ tablespoons sugar

Sift the flour, baking soda, baking powder and salt into a bowl and mix well. Beat 2 cups sugar and butter in a mixing bowl until creamy. Add the eggs 1 at a time, beating well after each addition. Add the flour mixture alternately with a mixture of the buttermilk and vanilla, mixing well after each addition. Spoon the batter into an 8×12-inch glass baking dish.

Bake at 350 degrees for 45 minutes. Combine the heavy cream and $2^1/_2$ tablespoons sugar in a saucepan. Cook until heated through, stirring occasionally; do not boil. Pour over the warm cake.

Serves 15

Versatile Cream Cheese Frosting

12 ounces cream cheese, softened
$^1/_4$ cup ($^1/_2$ stick) butter, softened
1 teaspoon vanilla extract
1 (1-pound) package confectioners' sugar, sifted
Milk

Combine the cream cheese and butter in a mixing bowl. Beat until creamy, scraping the bowl occasionally. Beat in the vanilla. Add the confectioners' sugar and beat until of a spreading consistency, adding milk 1 tablespoon at a time as needed for the desired consistency. Tint as desired with food coloring.

Makes enough frosting for one 2-layer cake or 2 dozen cupcakes

Rich Brownie Cupcakes

Cupcakes

1 cup flour
2 tablespoons baking cocoa
$^1/_8$ teaspoon salt
$^3/_4$ cup ($1^1/_2$ sticks) butter or margarine
2 ounces semisweet chocolate
1 ounce unsweetened chocolate
$1^3/_4$ cups sugar
4 eggs
1 teaspoon vanilla extract
1 cup chopped pecans, toasted

Filling

$^2/_3$ cup shortening
$^1/_2$ cup sugar
$^1/_3$ cup evaporated milk
1 tablespoon water
1 teaspoon vanilla extract
$^1/_4$ teaspoon salt
$^1/_2$ cup confectioners' sugar

For the cupcakes, combine the flour, baking cocoa and salt in a bowl and mix well. Combine the butter and chocolate in a saucepan. Cook over low heat until blended, stirring constantly. Remove from heat. Stir in the sugar. Add the eggs 1 at a time, mixing well after each addition. Stir in the vanilla. Add the flour mixture and whisk until smooth. Stir in the toasted pecans. Fill paper-lined muffin cups $^3/_4$ full. Bake at 350 degrees for 35 minutes.

For the filling, beat the shortening, sugar, evaporated milk, water, vanilla and salt in a mixing bowl for 8 to 10 minutes, scraping the bowl occasionally. Add the confectioners' sugar. Beat until creamy. Spoon the filling into a pastry tube fitted with a star tip. Squeeze the filling into the cupcakes.

Makes 16 cupcakes

Austin
Entertains
We hope you will, too!

Austin enjoys an eclectic mix of restaurants with a wide array of experienced and award-winning chefs. Many of these establishments reflect the multi-ethnic heritage of central Texas. The chefs on the following pages have generously given of their time and talents to provide us with these delicious recipes. Enjoy!

Eat Out, or Here's How to do it at Home!

1	Jeff Blank	Hudson's-on-the-Bend
2	Jay Moore	Hudson's-on-the-Bend
3	Patrick Dixson	Chez Zee Bistro Café
4	David Garrido	Jeffrey's
5	Alma Thomas	Jeffrey's
6	Daniel Haverty	Shoreline Grill
7	Tim Kartiganer	Chef's Table
8	Charles Mayes	Café Josie
9	Peter O'Brien	Si Bon
10	Roberto Santibañez	Fonda San Miguel
11	Kevin Williamson	Ranch 616
12	Mary Perna	Pastry Chef

Spicy Rosemary Shrimp with Ancho Bock Beer Smashed Potatoes

Chefs Jeff Blank and Jay Moore of Hudson's-on-the-Bend contributed this recipe.

2 cups (4 sticks) butter
3/4 cup chopped fresh rosemary
1/2 cup lemon juice
1/4 cup minced garlic
Grated zest of 3 lemons
2 bay leaves
2 tablespoons minced red onion
2 tablespoons paprika
2 teaspoons cracked black pepper
1 1/2 teaspoons cayenne pepper, or to taste
1 teaspoon salt
1/2 teaspoon dried oregano
1/2 teaspoon dried basil
2 pounds shrimp
1 recipe Ancho Bock Beer Smashed Potatoes (page 235)

Combine the butter, rosemary, lemon juice, garlic, lemon zest, bay leaves, onion, paprika, black pepper, cayenne pepper, salt, oregano and basil in a stockpot. Bring to a simmer. Simmer over low heat for 10 minutes, stirring occasionally. Add the shrimp. Increase the heat to medium-low.

Cook for 5 minutes or until the shrimp turn pink. Discard the bay leaves. Spoon the Ancho Bock Beer Smashed Potatoes onto a serving platter. Surround with the shrimp and sauce.

Serves 6 to 8

Ancho Bock Beer Smashed Potatoes

Chefs Jeff Blank and Jay Moore of Hudson's-on-the-Bend contributed this recipe.

5 or 6 ancho chiles
$1/2$ cup water
2 pounds Idaho baking potatoes, peeled
8 ounces sweet potatoes, peeled
1 cup (2 sticks) unsalted butter, cubed, softened
$1/2$ cup heavy cream, at room temperature
$1/2$ bottle Shiner Bock beer, or any malty beer,
 at room temperature
2 teaspoons salt

Combine the ancho chiles with enough water to cover in a bowl. Let stand until softened; drain. Chop the chiles, discarding the stems, seeds and membranes. Process the chiles with $1/2$ cup water in a blender until puréed, adding additional water if needed to yield $1/2$ cup.

Combine the baking potatoes and sweet potatoes in separate saucepans with enough water to cover. Bring to a boil. Boil until tender; drain.

Beat the baking potatoes and sweet potatoes in a mixing bowl until smooth. Add the butter 1 cube at a time, heavy cream, beer, salt and ancho purée, beating constantly until creamy. Add additional salt if needed. Cover to keep warm. If you need to reheat, add additional butter.

Serves 6 to 8

Char-Grilled Oysters on the Half Shell

Chef Patrick Dixson of Chez Zee Bistro Café contributed this recipe.

3 dozen unshucked oysters
2 cups (4 sticks) butter, softened
2 tablespoons minced garlic
1 tablespoon smoky roasted red bell pepper and garlic olive oil
1/2 teaspoon pepper
1/2 teaspoon grated Parmesan cheese
1/2 teaspoon grated Romano cheese
1/2 teaspoon chopped fresh parsley
1/2 teaspoon Melinda's habanero hot sauce

Split open the oysters. Combine the butter, garlic, olive oil, pepper, Parmesan cheese, Romano cheese, parsley and habanero hot sauce in a food processor. Process until blended. Spoon some of the butter mixture on top of each oyster on the half shell.

Arrange the half shells on a grill rack over an open char-grill flame. Grill until the shells become blackened on the bottom and the oysters are heated through. Serve hot with lemon wedges and an oyster fork. You will want to lick the shell!!

Serves 36

Parmesan Habanero Smoky Olive Oil Spread

Chef Patrick Dixson of Chez Zee Bistro Café contributed this recipe.

2 cups smoky roasted red bell pepper and garlic olive oil
1 cup shredded Parmesan cheese
1 tablespoon Melinda's habanero hot sauce, or to taste
Freshly ground pepper to taste
Coarse sea salt to taste

Mix the olive oil, cheese, hot sauce, pepper and sea salt in a bowl with a fork until of a chunky consistency. Serve with toasted Tuscan bread.

Serves 8 to 10

Zee Piña Colada Bread Pudding

Chef Patrick Dixson of Chez Zee Bistro Café contributed this recipe.

Bread Pudding
1 (15-ounce) can cream of coconut
2 cups cream
2 cups sugar
1^1/$_2$ cups chopped pecans, toasted
1 (8-ounce) can crushed pineapple
1 cup shredded coconut
^{1}/$_2$ cup (1 stick) butter, melted
3 eggs, lightly beaten
3 tablespoons vanilla extract
1 teaspoon cinnamon
^{1}/$_2$ teaspoon freshly ground nutmeg
1^1/$_2$ loaves dry French bread, cubed

Rum Sauce
1^1/$_2$ cups sugar
^{1}/$_2$ cup (1 stick) butter, melted
2 egg yolks, beaten
^{1}/$_2$ cup dark rum

For the bread pudding, combine the cream of coconut, cream, sugar, pecans, undrained pineapple, coconut, butter, eggs, vanilla, cinnamon and nutmeg in a bowl and mix well. Add the bread cubes and mix gently. Let stand until the bread soaks up the mixture, adding additional bread if needed; the mixture should not be runny. Spoon the bread mixture into a buttered baking pan. Bake at 350 degrees for 1 hour or until golden brown. Let stand until room temperature.

For the sauce, combine the sugar and butter in a saucepan. Cook over low heat until the sugar dissolves, stirring frequently. Remove from heat. Stir a small amount of the hot mixture into the egg yolks. Stir the egg yolks into the hot mixture. Add the rum gradually, stirring constantly until blended. Pour into a thermos to keep warm or place in a water bath.

To assemble, cut the bread pudding into 12 to 15 slices and arrange on dessert plates. Drizzle each serving with the warm sauce.

Serves 12 to 15

Crème Brûlée

Chef David Garrido of Jeffrey's contributed this recipe.

1 quart heavy cream
1 cup sugar
$^1/_2$ vanilla bean, split, scraped
3 tablespoons Bailey's Irish Cream
2 tablespoons Grand Marnier
$1^1/_2$ tablespoons amaretto
1 tablespoon espresso
$^1/_2$ cup packed brown sugar
7 egg yolks
2 eggs

Combine the heavy cream, $^1/_2$ cup of the sugar and vanilla bean in a saucepan. Cook over medium heat for 4 to 6 minutes or until the sugar dissolves and the mixture is heated through, stirring constantly. Remove from the heat. Stir in the Irish Cream, Grand Marnier, amaretto and espresso.

Whisk the brown sugar, egg yolks and eggs in a bowl. Stir 1 cup of the hot cream mixture into the egg mixture. Add the remaining hot cream mixture and mix well; strain. Pour the custard into 8 ramekins.

Bake in a water bath at 325 degrees for 30 to 40 minutes or until the custard is set but still quivers in the center. Cool on a wire rack for 30 minutes. Chill in the refrigerator. Sprinkle the top of each custard with 1 tablespoon of the remaining sugar. Using a propane torch, caramelize the top of each custard by heating the sugar until it turns dark amber in color. Garnish with fresh berries.

Serves 8

Pistachio Cookies

Chef David Garrido of Jeffrey's contributed this recipe.

1 cup (2 sticks) butter, softened
2^1/$_4$ cups packed brown sugar
1^3/$_4$ cups sugar
2 eggs
5 cups cake flour
1 tablespoon baking powder
1 tablespoon baking soda
10 ounces shredded coconut
2 cups pistachios
4 cups cornflakes, crushed

Beat the butter, brown sugar and sugar in a mixing bowl until creamy. Add the eggs and beat until blended. Combine the cake flour, baking powder and baking soda in a bowl and mix well. Add to the creamed mixture and mix well. Beat in the coconut, pistachios and cornflakes.

Shape the dough into logs. Chill, wrapped in plastic wrap, until firm. Cut each log into slices. Arrange the slices on nonstick cookie sheets. Bake at 325 degrees for 18 to 20 minutes or until light brown. Cool on the cookie sheets for 2 minutes. Remove to a wire rack to cool completely.

Makes 3 dozen large cookies

Pepper-Seared Rib-Eyes with Gorgonzola Compound Butter and Warm Apple Bacon Potato Salad

Chef Daniel Haverty of Shoreline Grill contributed this recipe.

Gorgonzola Compound Butter

1 pound whipped butter
12 ounces Gorgonzola cheese
3 tablespoons roasted garlic
1 tablespoon chopped fresh oregano

1 teaspoon freshly ground white
 pepper
Kosher salt to taste

Apple Bacon Potato Salad

2 Idaho potatoes, cut into
 1/2-inch pieces
4 ounces apple bacon, julienned
1 red onion, julienned

2 ribs celery, diagonally sliced
1/4 cup Champagne vinegar
Kosher salt and white pepper to taste

Sherry Demi-Glace

4 garlic cloves, minced
1 tablespoon peppercorns
Butter

1/2 cup sherry
8 ounces demi-glace
Kosher salt to taste

Rib-Eye Steaks

4 rib-eye steaks
Kosher salt to taste

Freshly cracked pepper

For the butter, combine the whipped butter, cheese, roasted garlic, oregano, white pepper and kosher salt in a mixing bowl fitted with a paddle attachment. Beat until blended.

For the potato salad, combine the potatoes with enough water to cover in a saucepan. Bring to a boil. Boil until tender; drain. Let stand until cool. Fry the bacon in a skillet until crisp; drain. Combine the potatoes, bacon, onion, celery, vinegar, kosher salt and white pepper in a bowl and toss gently to mix.

For the demi-glace, sauté the garlic and peppercorns in a small amount of butter in a skillet until the garlic is light brown. Stir in the sherry. Cook until most of the liquid has been absorbed, stirring frequently. Stir in the demi-glace. Season with kosher salt.

For the rib-eyes, sprinkle the rib-eyes with kosher salt and pepper. Sear in a cast-iron skillet for 30 seconds on each side. Bake in a hot oven until of the desired degree of doneness.

To assemble, heat the potato salad in the demi-glace in a saucepan. Spoon the potato salad evenly onto 4 serving plates. Arrange the steaks over the potato salad. Top each steak with some of the butter.

Serves 4

Grand Marnier Ricotta Cheesecake

Chef Tim Kartiganer of the Chef's Table contributed this recipe.

Crust
   3 cups graham cracker crumbs
   $1/2$ cup (1 stick) butter, softened
   $1/4$ cup sugar

Filling
   16 ounces cream cheese, softened
   $3/4$ cup sugar
   3 eggs
   1 cup cream
   $1/2$ cup ricotta cheese
   $1/2$ cup sour cream
   1 vanilla bean, split and scraped
   2 tablespoons Grand Marnier
   1 tablespoon grated orange zest

For the crust, process the graham cracker crumbs, butter and sugar in a food processor until crumbly. Press the crumb mixture over the bottom and up the side of a 9-inch cake pan.

For the filling, beat the cream cheese and sugar in a mixing bowl at medium speed until creamy. Add the eggs 1 at a time, beating well after each addition. Add the cream, ricotta cheese, sour cream, vanilla bean, Grand Marnier and orange zest. Beat at low speed until mixed.

Spoon the filling into the prepared pan. Bake in a water bath at 325 degrees for 1 hour. Remove from the water bath. Let stand until cool. Chill, covered, for 4 to 10 hours. Remove to a serving platter.

Serves 12

Grilled Crawfish Quesadillas

Chef Charles Mayes of Café Josie contributed this recipe.

Smokin' Chipotle Hot Sauce
1 can chipotle chiles
$1/2$ chile can cider vinegar
$1/2$ chile can water

Crawfish Quesadillas
1 pound cooked crawfish tails
Seasoned salt to taste
20 flour tortillas
1 pound white Cheddar cheese, shredded
1 ear of corn, grilled, cut from cob
1 fire-roasted poblano chile, chopped
1 fire-roasted red bell pepper, chopped
Vegetable oil

For the sauce, process the chiles, vinegar and water in a blender until puréed.

For the quesadillas, sprinkle the crawfish tails with seasoned salt. Grill over hot coals. Arrange 10 of the tortillas on a hard clean surface. Sprinkle each tortilla with a thin layer of the cheese, corn, poblano chile and bell pepper. Layer with the crawfish tails and remaining cheese. Top each with 1 of the remaining tortillas. You may prepare the quesadillas in advance up to this point and store, covered, in the refrigerator for several hours.

Heat a cast-iron skillet until hot. Coat the surface of the skillet with a small amount of oil. Brown the quesadillas in batches in the skillet, turning once. Cut into wedges. Serve immediately with the sauce.

Serves 12 to 15

Lobster Corn Pudding with Key Lime Fraîche

Chef Charles Mayes of Café Josie contributed this recipe.

Key Lime Fraîche
1 cup plain yogurt
1 cup heavy cream
Juice of 2 Key limes

$1/8$ teaspoon salt
$1/8$ teaspoon sugar

Corn Pudding
6 cups whole kernel corn
8 egg yolks
$1/4$ cup ($1/2$ stick) butter, melted
Juice of 1 lime
$1/2$ cup wheat flour
$1/2$ cup corn flour
3 tablespoons sugar
1 teaspoon salt

1 teaspoon baking powder
2 cups shredded cotija cheese
1 poblano chile, minced
1 red bell pepper, minced
1 sprig of cilantro, chopped
1 pound lobster meat, chopped
8 egg whites

For the lime fraîche, combine the yogurt, heavy cream, lime juice, salt and sugar in a bowl and mix gently. Let stand at room temperature for 1 to 2 hours. Chill, covered, in the refrigerator.

For the pudding, combine the corn, egg yolks, butter and lime juice in a food processor. Pulse until puréed. Combine the wheat flour, corn flour, sugar, salt and baking powder in a bowl and mix well. Stir the purée, cheese, poblano chile, bell pepper and cilantro into the flour mixture. Fold in the lobster meat. Whisk the egg whites in a bowl until foamy. Fold into the lobster mixture. Spoon into a buttered 9×13-inch baking pan. Bake at 350 degrees for 50 to 60 minutes or until light brown and the center is almost set. Let stand for 10 to 15 minutes to set. Serve with the lime fraîche.

Serves 6 to 8

Smoked Pheasant, Celery Root, Fennel and Apple Salad

Chef Peter O'Brien of Si Bon contributed this recipe.

2 Granny Smith apples, peeled, julienned
1 small celery root, peeled, julienned
Lemon juice
$1/2$ fennel bulb
4 cups julienned smoked pheasant, chicken or turkey
1 cup golden raisins
Grated zest of 1 lemon
Grated zest of 1 orange
2 tablespoons chopped fresh tarragon
1 tablespoon finely chopped shallots
$1/2$ cup mayonnaise
3 tablespoons Dijon mustard
2 teaspoons Cognac
Salt and pepper to taste
Butter lettuce

Combine the apples and celery root with a mixture of lemon juice and water in a bowl and mix well. Remove the core of the fennel bulb and slice the fennel into long strips from the top to the bottom. Drain the apples and celery root.

Combine the apples, celery root, fennel, pheasant, raisins, lemon zest, orange zest, tarragon and shallots in a bowl and mix well. Stir in a mixture of the mayonnaise, Dijon mustard and Cognac. Season with salt and pepper. Spoon the salad into butter lettuce cups on serving plates.

Serves 4 to 6

Chilled Tomato Soup

Chef Peter O'Brien of Si Bon contributed this recipe.

1 teaspoon finely chopped shallot
1 teaspoon finely chopped garlic
1 teaspoon finely chopped fresh rosemary
1 teaspoon finely chopped fresh oregano
1 teaspoon finely chopped fresh thyme
1 teaspoon finely chopped anchovy
2 tablespoons olive oil
2 tablespoons tomato paste, caramelized
2 cups chopped seeded peeled Roma tomatoes
1 cup chicken stock
Salt and pepper to taste
2 cups heavy cream
$1/4$ cup soy sauce

Sweat the shallot, garlic, rosemary, oregano, thyme and anchovy in the olive oil in a 3-quart saucepan. Stir in the tomato paste. Add the tomatoes and stock and mix well. Season with salt and pepper.

Simmer for 40 minutes, stirring occasionally. Chill in an ice bath. Stir in the heavy cream and soy sauce. Ladle into chilled soup bowls.

Serves 4 to 6

Chiles Anchos Rellenos de Picadillo de Pollo

Chef Roberto Santibañez of Fonda San Miguel contributed this recipe.

Picadillo

1/4 cup mild olive oil
1 cup finely chopped Mexican white onion
2 tablespoons minced garlic
4 cups finely chopped Roma tomatoes
2 small bay leaves
1/4 teaspoon dried thyme
1/2 cup manzanilla olives, coarsely chopped
1/2 cup raisins
1/4 cup capers, rinsed

1/4 cup mild olive oil
2 pounds chicken, finely chopped or coarsely ground
Salt to taste
1/2 cup slivered almonds
1/4 cup packed cilantro leaves, finely chopped
1/4 cup packed parsley leaves, finely chopped
6 mint leaves, finely chopped

Chiles

4 cups water
4 ounces piloncillo, grated
2/3 cup cider vinegar

1 (1/2-inch) piece cinnamon bark
1/2 teaspoon salt
8 to 10 ancho chiles, slit, seeded

Cilantro Sauce

2 cups crème fraîche or Mexican crème
1/2 cup finely chopped Mexican white onion

1/4 cup packed cilantro leaves, finely chopped
1/2 teaspoon coarse sea salt

For the picadillo, heat 1/4 cup olive oil in a saucepan. Add the onion. Cook for 2 minutes or until tender, stirring frequently. Stir in the garlic. Cook for 1 minute. Add the tomatoes, bay leaves and thyme. Boil over medium heat for 15 minutes. Stir in the olives, raisins and capers. Cook for 10 minutes longer. Heat 1/4 cup olive oil in a sauté pan over high heat until the olive oil smokes. Stir in the chicken. Cook until cooked through, stirring constantly. Season with salt. Stir in the tomato mixture. Bring to a boil. Boil for 5 minutes. Stir in the almonds, cilantro, parsley and mint. Let stand until cool. Discard the bay leaves.

For the chiles, combine the first 5 ingredients in a saucepan. Bring to a boil; reduce heat. Simmer for 5 minutes. Add the ancho chiles and cover. Remove from heat. Let stand for 8 minutes. Remove the chiles to a paper towel to drain. Stuff the chiles with the picadillo. Arrange in a single layer in an ovenproof earthenware dish. Bake, covered, at 350 to 400 degrees for 15 minutes or until heated through.

For the sauce, combine the crème fraîche and onion in a saucepan. Bring to a boil. Boil for 8 minutes; strain. Stir in the cilantro and sea salt. Cover to keep warm.

To assemble, arrange the chiles on 4 or 5 serving plates. Drizzle with the sauce. Garnish with hot cooked white rice and black beans.

Serves 4 or 5

Ancho Honey Glaze

Chef Kevin Williamson of Ranch 616 contributed this recipe.

8 ancho chiles, chopped
6 garlic cloves, minced
1/2 small yellow onion, chopped

White wine
4 cups honey

Combine the ancho chiles, garlic and onion in a saucepan and mix well. Add just enough white wine to cover. Simmer until the wine evaporates, stirring occasionally. Stir in the honey. Cook just until the mixture comes to a simmer, stirring frequently.

Makes 4 to 5 cups

Tomatillo Sauce

Chef Kevin Williamson of Ranch 616 contributed this recipe.

8 pounds tomatillos, peeled
1/4 cup vegetable oil
4 jalapeño chiles
6 garlic cloves, minced

Salt and pepper to taste
1 bunch cilantro, minced
Juice of 2 limes

Combine the tomatillos, oil, jalapeño chiles, garlic, salt and pepper in a saucepan. Cook, covered, over medium heat until the tomatillos and jalapeño chiles are tender, stirring occasionally. Pour the tomatillo mixture into a blender. Add the cilantro and lime juice. Process until puréed.

Makes 16 cups

Sugar Cure

Chef Kevin Williamson of Ranch 616 contributed this recipe.

1 cup sugar
1 cup packed brown sugar
1/2 cup chile powder
1/2 cup paprika

1/4 cup each dried basil, thyme,
   oregano and cayenne pepper
1/4 cup garlic powder
1/4 cup each dry mustard and salt

Mix the sugar, brown sugar, chile powder, paprika, basil, thyme, oregano, cayenne pepper, garlic powder, dry mustard and salt in a bowl. Store in an airtight container.

Makes 4 3/4 cups

Recipe Contributors and Testers

Kristin DeMallie Alleman
Pamela Z. Allen
Pamela Lee Allen
Lisa Alverson
Lori Askew
Elizabeth Ateyeh
Sara H. Atkins
Susan Avant
Heatherly Ayres
Julie Ayres
Leslie Bagby
Meghan Bailey
Emily Baker
Suzy Balagia
Leslie Ballanfonte
Julie Ballard
Martha Banister
Dinah Barksdale
Donna Barksdale
Kelly Barnhill
Jamie Barshop
Jan Bashur
Christine Baskin
Jan Bates
Candy Gray Becker
Yuniedith Bennett
Elizabeth Look Biar
Rebecca Biehunko
Linda Biel
Bobby Bigsby
Maya Bledsoe
Anne E. Bloomer
Karen Boatright
Laura Bohls
Leigh Ann Bonham
Corrinne Bowers
Scott Boyd
Tam Braithwaite
Katie Breihan
Jeri Brock
Carrie Brown
Sheryl Brown
Benie Bruner

Laura Bush
Catherine Camillone
Alison Campbell
Donna Campbell
Gretchen Canter
Dannielle Cantrell
Mindy Meadows Carr
Laura Caskey
Theresa Catalani
Susan Chambers
Gail Chavez
Valerie Cheney
Roseann Ciani
Nancy Clark
Elizabeth Coffin
Benie Colvin
Elizabeth Colvin
Ashley Copeland
Jean Cornett
Cathy Cour
Martha Covert
Carol Crowley
Andrea Crowson
Carol Darilek
Miranda Guidry Darr
Jenefred Davies
Tanya Davis
Kim Day
Sarah Devries
Nancy Dishong
Diana Dobson
Dawnelle Doughtie
Michelle Drajeske
Paula Reinemund Duke
Amy Dunham
Jean Kellner Durkee
Lea Easter
Louise Eckelman
Leslie Eckert
Nancy Edsel
Bonny Edwards
Melissa Edwards
Lori Eidenschink

Molly Drake Elder
Martha Ernst
Rhonda Erwin
Eledith Falk
Diane Falkenberg
Kathy Farr
Joan Felton
Dot Fields
Suzy M. Fields
Ann Finley
Janet Fish
Patty Flack
Janelle Foster
Ruth Frye-Harper
Gay Gaddis
Meredith Garcia
Nancy Garrison
Melanie Gaylord
Elizabeth Lawrence Gillies
Kristen Goen
Jana Lee Gondran
Kelly Goulding
Catherine Graves
Staley Gray
Lizz Cavanaugh Grimes
Cordie Brunson Grosvenor
Jennifer Gunnin
Mary Lou Gwynn
Clarkie Hall
Alice Hamilton
Claire Hamilton
Susan E. Harbin
Micki Harlow
Sally Harner
Jane Morriss Harrison
Stefania Rigo Haustein
Jere Hayden
Amy Hellmund
Jean D. Hendrix
Holli Hill
Nancy Hilliard
Patti Hirsch
Nora Hodges

Amy Hohmann
Loretta Holland
Elizabeth Holt
Nancy Hoover
Lisa Hostetler
May Howard
Jana Howden
Rebecca Hudson
Hayley Hughes
Ellen Humoert
Jeannie Hatch Hutchison
Nikki Jackson
Lisa Jardine
Elizabeth Jeffers
Michelle Johnson
Bettsy Culbertson Jones
Brenda Jones
Kim Cook Jones
Silver Jones
Lynn P. Jordan
Beth Jouett
Karen Kahan
Judy Louise Karcher
Susan G. Kay
Andrew Keever
Sonja Keever
Kristie Kelly
Tina Kemmerer
Betsy Kirksey
Laura Kooris
Sheri Krause
April Kubik
Mary Ann Kuhlmann
Hazel Lacy
Ashley Larkin
Jodi Leach
Robin Levatino
Annabel Linscomb
Leah Lloyd
Kathy Lockart
Polly Lucas
Kathy Madden
Tiffany Mahaffee
Sharon Malone
Mary Ann Maltz
Christine Dool Malvezzi
Mary Frances Markley

Laura Mauro
Connie Maverick
Nancy McAllister
Melissa McAnelly
Pat McAnelly
Marilyn M. McDonald
Vicki Mechling
Marcella Medford
Margie Mellick
Christy Allen Merritt
Margaret Michelanger
Ceci Miglicco
Eugenia Miller
Lorraine Miller
Jackie Milstead
Phyllis Milstead
Sandra Moore
Cindy Moreland
Sharon Morris
Verna Mae Morrison
Melissa Greenwood Morrow
Jennifer Mouritsen
Elizabeth Murphy
Carole Nalle
Frances Netherton
Lucy Netherton
Lavon Neumann
Kathryn Newth
Stacey Nicchio
Hallie Nikotich
Georgia Trapp Nolan
Cathy Northcutt
Dina Northington
Patti Obenhaus
Dee Oberwetter
Donna Olmstead
Carol Onion
Karen Oswalt
Shelly Ozdil
Beth Ozmun
Dorothy B. Painter
Mary Jane Parker
Susan Parker
Sherri Patten
Valerie Shank Paul
Jennifer Peters
Gina Pickard

Peggy Pickle
Lynn Pollinger
Barb Powell
Nancy Prideaux
Sherri Pullen
Cindy Hoenig Purcell
Meg Putman
Cile Ramey
Annette Ramey-Graf
MariBen Ramsey
Suzy Ranney
Sharman Reed
Jenifer Regan
Ferree Foy Rhodes
Cindy Richter
Polly Rickard
Erin Rippert
Shannon Robertson
Lisa Fowler Rodman
Christine Ryan
Carole Keeton Rylander
Ellie Schneider
Susie Schumacher
Kathy Schwartz
Aileen Secunda
Rena Sehlke
Camille Shannon
Linda Shaunessy
Lesa Shaw
Renee Shilling
Shay Wade Shoop
Caryn Short
Dana Sipes
Beth Smith
Chuchu Waltmon Smith
Elora Smith
Fraser Smith
Katherine Smith
Lanette Smith
Lynn Smith
Pat Smith
Sara Smith
Sue Brantley Smith
Suzy Smith
Carla Smyrl
Doug Snyder
Lori Snyder

Tracey Sorenson
Jennifer Stewart
Andrea Stidham
Carol Strickland
Cindy Sullivan
Frances Swanson
Judy Talbot
Joan Granger Talley
Jennifer Taylor
Marilyn Tankersley Taylor
Robin Thomas
Sabrina Thomas
Jean Powell Thompson
Mary Lib Thornhill
Leslie Timmerman
Anne Tounget
Cassie Maddox Townsend
Lisa Trahan
Deidre Vedder
Gayle Vickers
Leslie Vogl
Terri Von Dohlen
Lori Voyles
Pat Wallace
Molly Watson
Kristin Weatherspoon
Tracy Wehmeyer
Hannah Weldon
Holly White
Pam M. White
Pam Doster Whitley
Jane Turner Wicker
Ann Lindsay Wilhelm
Denise Williams
Marilyn Willson
Cathy Wilson
Laura Wolf
Vanessa Wolfe
Kathleen Wood
Meredith Wood
Mary Trapp Woodruff
Camille Yale
Ellen Yaun
Coralinn Young
Margee Young

Index

The Junior League of Austin Cookbooks

5416 Parkcrest, Suite 100

Austin, Texas 78731

Telephone: 1-888-903-0888 or 1-512-467-9455

Fax: 1-512-454-7518

Email: cookbook@jlaustin.org

Website: www.jlaustin.org

Name

Street Address

| City | State | Zip |

Telephone   Email (optional)

Your Order	Quantity	Total
Austin Entertains at $28.95 per book		$
Necessities and Temptations at $19.95 per book		$
The Collection at $19.95 per book		$
Shipping and handling at $4.00 per book		$
Total		$

Method of Payment: [   ] VISA   [   ] MasterCard

[   ] Check payable to The Junior League of Austin Cookbooks

Account Number   Expiration Date

Cardholder Name

Signature

Photocopies accepted.